About IFPRI

The International Food Policy Research Institute (IFPRI®) was established in 1975 to identify and analyze alternative national and international strategies and policies for meeting food needs of the developing world on a sustainable basis, with particular emphasis on low-income countries and on the poorer groups in those countries. While the research effort is geared to the precise objective of contributing to the reduction of hunger and malnutrition, the factors involved are many and wide-ranging, requiring analysis of underlying processes and extending beyond a narrowly defined food sector. The Institute's research program reflects worldwide collaboration with governments and private and public institutions interested in increasing food production and improving the equity of its distribution. Research results are disseminated to policymakers, opinion formers, administrators, policy analysts, researchers, and others concerned with national and international food and agricultural policy.

About IFPRI Research Monographs

IFPRI Research Monographs are well-focused, policy-relevant monographs based on original and innovative research conducted at IFPRI. All manuscripts submitted for publication as IFPRI Research Monographs undergo extensive external and internal reviews. Prior to submission to the Publications Review Committee, each manuscript is circulated informally among the author's colleagues. Upon submission to the Committee, the manuscript is reviewed by an IFPRI reviewer and presented in a formal seminar. Three additional reviewers—at least two external to IFPRI and one from the Committee—are selected to review the manuscript. Reviewers are chosen for their familiarity with the country setting. The Committee provides the author its reaction to the reviewers' comments. After revising as necessary, the author resubmits the manuscript to the Committee with a written response to the reviewers' and Committee's comments. The Committee then makes its recommendations on publication of the manuscript to the Director General of IFPRI. With the Director General's approval, the manuscript becomes part of the IFPRI Research Monograph series. The publication series, under the original name of IFPRI Research Reports, began in 1977.

A New Era of Transformation in Ghana

Lessons from the Past and Scenarios for the Future

Clemens Breisinger, Xinshen Diao, Shashidhara Kolavalli, Ramatu Al Hassan, and James Thurlow

RESEARCH MONOGRAPH

INTERNATIONAL FOOD POLICY
RESEARCH INSTITUTE
sustainable solutions for ending hunger and poverty

Supported by the CGIAR

International Food Policy Research Institute
2033 K Street, NW
Washington, D.C. 20006-1002, U.S.A.
Telephone +1-202-862-5600
www.ifpri.org

DOI: 10.2499/9780896297883

Library of Congress Cataloging-in-Publication Data

A new era of transformation in Ghana : lessons from the past and
scenarios for the future / Clemens Breisinger . . . [et al.].
    p.   cm. — (IFPRI research monograph)
  Includes bibliographical references and index.
  ISBN 978-0-89629-788-3 (alk. paper)
  1. Economic development—Ghana.   2. Ghana—Economic conditions.
3. Agriculture—Economic aspects—Ghana.   I. Breisinger, Clemens.
II. Series: IFPRI research monograph.
HC1060.N47   2011
330.9667—dc22   2010042114

Contents

Tables

Figures

Boxes

Foreword

C ountries such as Brazil, China, and India have demonstrated in the past two decades that poverty can be reduced through rapid economic transformation. African countries have also made unprecedented progress in growth and poverty reduction over the past decade, but more needs to be done to match the recent successes of Asian and Latin American countries. Many African countries still suffer from low levels of economic diversification, high dependency on a few primary commodity exports, failure to tap significant agricultural potential, and high levels of poverty. Identifying why these challenges persist will help policymakers develop strategies and investment priorities that accelerate both economic transformation and poverty reduction, thereby improving the lives of millions of Africans.

To accomplish this, the authors of this research monograph provide an in-depth account of Ghana's economic development, as well as models of the Ghanaian economy, which they examine in the context of broader economic history and an analysis of structural change in other countries. The authors argue that economic transformation theory—which currently defines transformation as a country's shift from a rural, agriculture-based economy to an urban, industrialized economy—should be broadened to include such considerations as the distribution of wealth and the level of poverty. A simple shift from rural to urban and agriculture to industry may bring growth to some and leave others behind. Wealth distribution and poverty levels critically depend on the type and sources of growth. The authors' research clearly shows that agriculture and "homegrown" manufacturing sectors are more likely to foster sustained job-creating and poverty-reducing growth. Achieving such growth predominantly through private-sector leadership and in a way consistent with countries' comparative advantage is likely to require a greater degree of government involvement than called for in "Washington consensus"-style policy prescriptions. Crucial ingredients in the required government strategy are promoting a good investment climate and providing the necessary institutional and physical infrastructure in rural and urban areas.

Ghana has often been an economic frontrunner in African history, so Ghanaians increasingly ask why their country has fallen so far behind countries like South Korea, which in the 1960s had a per capita income comparable to Ghana's. The authors show that, consistent with the Ghanaian mood, government strategy is moving toward a more coordinated and outcome-oriented approach. Much can be learned from Asian and Latin American success stories, yet the authors point out the importance of accounting for local and country-specific conditions. For example, given Ghana's huge untapped agricultural potential and the projected large rises in domestic and global demand for food, agricultural development is likely to play a bigger role in economic transformation and poverty reduction in Ghana than elsewhere. If Ghana and other Sub-Saharan African countries continue their current reforms and take advantage of the major opportunities available to them, there is little doubt they will catch up with other world regions sooner rather than later.

Shenggen Fan
Director General, International Food Policy Research Institute

Acknowledgments

This research monograph is a product of several related research projects under IFPRI's Ghana Strategy Support Program (GSSP). Many people have contributed to the development of this monograph, to all of whom we express our deepest gratitude for their support.

We first thank all our Ghanaian collaborators for their invaluable contributions, comments, and provision of data. We especially thank Professor Gyan-Baffour, Ministry of Finance and Economic Planning (MoFEP); Dr. Regina Adutwum, National Development Planning Commission (NDPC); and all the members of GSSP's national supervisory board for their continued support for the program. We are grateful to Professor N. N. N. Nsowah-Nuamah and to Magnus Duncan, both of Ghana Statistical Services (GSS), for providing access to various country data sources, many fruitful discussions on data quality, and extensive support for database improvements. We are also grateful to Dr. Aggrey Fynn and Lena Otoo, both of the Ministry of Food and Agriculture (MoFA), and their staff for access to agricultural production and trade data and for their personal reflections on Ghana's agricultural development history. We also thank the Ghana modeling team, led by Dr. Amuzu and (since 2008) by Dr. Alhassan (both of MoFEP), and staff at the Bank of Ghana, MoFEP, NDPC, GSS, and the University of Ghana for discussions during several training workshops.

Many parts of this monograph have been presented at various policy workshops and international academic conferences. We thank participants in IFPRI's Ghana Strategy Forum held in Accra in November 2007, especially Minister of Agriculture Ernest Debrah and Deputy Minister of Finance and Planning Professor George Gyan-Baffour, for their insightful speeches and workshop contributions. We also thank participants in the Agricultural Sector Planning Group, including representatives of MoFA, the Ministry of Transport, the Ministry of Local Governance, the Ghana Irrigation Authority, and others, for their useful comments and suggestions during the Comprehensive Africa Agriculture Development Programme (CAADP) planning workshop in Accra in May 2008. We further thank all participants in the American Agricultural Economics Association; Poverty Reduction, Equity and Growth Network; and Tropentag conferences, at which different parts of the monograph have been presented. We also thank Lothar Diehl, German Agency for Technical

Cooperation (GTZ), Ghana; Chris Jackson, World Bank, Ghana; and the United States Agency for International Development (USAID) Ghana team for stimulating discussions.

We have also benefited from the valuable comments and suggestions of colleagues at IFPRI, including Ousmane Badiane, Sam Benin, Regina Birner, Shenggen Fan, Derek Headey, Michael Johnson, Tewodaj Mogues, Sam Morley, Alejandro Nin-Pratt, John Ulimwengu, Bingxin Yu, Xiaobo Zhang, and many others. We are especially indebted to Afua Banful, who provided important input to the monograph, especially on Ghana's economic history. We also thank Terry Roe and Franz Heidhues for their suggestions at the early stages of this research, as well as Jørn Rattsø, Terry Roe, Isabelle Tsakok, and several anonymous reviewers who provided detailed comments and valuable suggestions on earlier drafts of different parts of this monograph.

Funding for this research has been provided by USAID through its support of GSSP, by the World Bank through its 2007 Country Economic Memorandum, and by GTZ, which has provided financial support.

Acronyms and Abbreviations

ABS	average budget share
CAADP	Comprehensive Africa Agriculture Development Programme
C-D	Cobb-Douglas
CES	constant elasticity of substitution
CGE	computable general equilibrium
CV	coefficient variation
DCGE	dynamic computable general equilibrium
ERP	Economic Recovery Program
FAO	Food and Agriculture Organization of the United Nations
FDI	foreign direct investment
FOB	free on board
GDP	gross domestic product
GLSS5	2005–06 Ghana Living Standards Survey
GNI	gross national income
GPRS II	Second Growth and Poverty Reduction Strategy
GSS	Ghana Statistical Services
GSSP	Ghana Strategy Support Program
HIPC	Heavily Indebted Poor Countries
IMF	International Monetary Fund
ISI	import substitution industrialization
MBS	marginal budget share
MDG 1	Millennium Development Goal 1
MIC	middle-income country
MoFA	Ministry of Food and Agriculture
MoFEP	Ministry of Finance and Economic Planning
NDPC	National Development Planning Commission
NEPAD	New Partnership for Africa's Development
NGO	nongovernmental organization

SAM   social accounting matrix

SAP   structural adjustment program

SME   small and medium-sized enterprise

SOE   state-owned enterprise

TFP   total factor productivity

USAID   United States Agency for International Development

Summary

After decades of rapid income divergence between Africa and the rest of the world, a new era of change has come to several African countries. This new era is characterized by macroeconomic stabilization, sustained growth, and improved governance, which mark a historic break from decades of economic stagnation and political turmoil. Therefore, there is now a unique opportunity for the front-running African countries to set examples on how to achieve economic transformation and prosperity on the continent. This is especially important because the initial conditions of African economies and societies are markedly different from those of most countries in other regions of the world. These differences will likely have consequences for the paths of economic transformation, which might also suggest that African transformation might differ from experiences in other regions of the world.

Ghana is a prime candidate to champion economic transformation in Africa. Ghana has experienced two decades of sound and persistent annual growth of around 5 percent and is bound to become the first Sub-Saharan African country to achieve the first Millennium Development Goal (MDG 1) of halving poverty before the target year, 2015. Ghana has made rapid progress in state and institution building and has become a stable democratic state. Perhaps most important, Ghanaians have realized their economic potential and are determined to catch up to countries in Asia that have been successful in transforming themselves, such as Malaysia and Thailand, which started out in the late 1960s at per capita income levels lower than Ghana's today.

To assess possible transformation paths and opportunities for rapid development, this research monograph first synthesizes the process and characteristics of economic transformation based on a broad literature review and broad lessons drawn from selected successfully transforming countries. The monograph also provides a description of the lessons drawn from Ghana's own economic history. Based on these descriptive analyses the monograph develops a highly disaggregated dynamic general equilibrium model and applies this model to assess Ghana's growth options in transformation with special attention to the role of agriculture and Green Revolution–type growth.

The findings of the monograph can be summarized as follows. Setting ambitious development visions and goals is necessary to catch up with the frontrunners of development. Yet in the past the governments of Ghana have often been too ambitious and unfocused in pursuing their goals, and there has often been a rush to claim success. More recently, the country has made great progress in setting more realistic development goals that are adapted to local conditions and supported by evidence-based assessments. The modeling analysis of this monograph indicates that Ghana can achieve two of its major development goals: reaching the status of a middle-income country (MIC) and halving its poverty level of the 1990s in a period of 10–15 years.

Political, institutional, and macroeconomic stability are key for rapid economic transformation. In Ghana, decades of political instability in the past delayed a shift away from state-led industrialization strategies and deteriorated institutional memory and capacity. Moreover, the state-led approach contributed to the rapid rise of macroeconomic imbalances and vicious circles of policies impedimental to modernization. In the two most recent decades, the return of confidence in the country's creditworthiness and the perspectives for both private and public investments have been promising. Ghana is no longer seen as a country "where investment may prosper under one regime at best, but could not be guaranteed under the next one" (Gyimah-Boadi 2008, 223).

The private sector has an important role to play in economic transformation. Manufacturing has been regarded as the main driver of this process both in early development theory and in successful countries' practice. Although manufacturing growth should be led by the private sector, support from the government through policies and public investment is equally important. Experiences from Asian countries have shown that "homegrown" manufacturing and services are likely to be more consistent with a country's initial conditions and able to take advantage of the country's comparative advantages; hence, they can lead to broad-based growth.

Strengthening productivity-led growth and growth linkages is key for accelerating transformation. Although innovations have often been prevented by a system of political patronage in the past, improved political transparency and the spread of information technology are likely to increase the incentives for the private sector to lead growth. In this process, expatriate Ghanaians can play an increasingly important role in innovation, and many have already done so (Ofori-Atta 2008). Potentials for productivity-led growth exist. For example, under certain conditions traditional homegrown manufacturing can be transformed into a modern sector, while large yield gaps in agriculture suggest great potentials for productivity-led Green Revolution–type growth.

Although manufacturing has been the main driver of transformation in the practice of other successful countries, the initial conditions of manufacturing in Ghana limit the sector's role in transformation. The modeling analysis in this monograph shows that the capacity of the manufacturing sector in

Ghana to grow rapidly is constrained by agricultural and rural income growth, which supports manufacturing growth by providing cheap raw materials and expanded domestic market opportunities. A significant departure of manufacturing and agricultural growth thus relies on the emergence of export-oriented manufacturing that is labor intensive and less reliant on agricultural material inputs.

The service sector is expected to play a supporting role in Ghana's transformation. Although the country undoubtedly has the potential to expand its export services and provide substitutes for imported services, the extremely small initial size of this subsector limits its role in early transformation. Even if the growth rate of Ghana's export services were to match that of India, the modeling analysis indicates that the export services in their current form are unlikely to engender significant structural transformation. Yet domestic services, especially the trade and transport sectors, can stimulate growth through their strong linkages with the rest of the economy. Indeed, China and Thailand have experienced more rapid service-sector growth alongside industry-led transformations.

In the early stage of development, broad-based agricultural development is key for transformation. Accelerating agricultural growth is a must for Ghana to reach the MIC target. Ghana's agricultural development in the past has often narrowly focused on foreign exchange earnings from cocoa and promotion of large-scale farming. Experience from all successfully transforming countries suggests that agricultural growth must be broad based. The modeling analysis of this monograph shows that by closing the existing yield gaps for major staple crops together with achieving comparable productivity growth in the livestock sector, Ghana will be able to reach an average annual agricultural growth rate of 6 percent over the next 10 to 15 years, a growth rate consistent with the CAADP goal set by African policymakers. The Green Revolution type of agriculture benefits the whole economy through strong linkages between the agricultural sector and the rest of the economy. In this process, incomes of both rural and urban households increase and the resulting additional demand for agricultural products can be met by domestic supply without significantly lowering their prices. Green Revolution–type growth is also pro-poor. At the national level, this scenario shows that the national poverty rate will fall to 12.5 percent by 2015, lifting an additional 850,000 people out of poverty compared to the baseline. However, poverty levels in North Ghana will remain high, indicating the need for additional target measures beyond those of the Green Revolution.

Achieving a Green Revolution requires significant increases in public investments in agriculture. This monograph provides analytic evidence to support such investment. By taking into account both visible and invisible transfers from agriculture to the nonagricultural economy, the modeling analysis shows that Green Revolution-type agricultural growth will provide huge benefits to the economy. Financial transfers (in monetary terms) from agriculture to the rest of the economy will be equivalent to 18 percent of increased total gross domestic product (GDP) in the next 13 years, and invisible transfers such as those achieved through lowering food prices will be the dominant sources of this substantial contribution.

CHAPTER 1

Introduction

Background

After decades of rapid income divergence between Africa and the rest of the world, a new era of change has come to several African countries. This new era is characterized by macroeconomic stabilization, sustained growth, and improved governance and marks a historic break from decades of growing internal and external deficits, economic stagnation, and political turmoil.[1] It is therefore a time of unique opportunity for Africa, and the frontrunners in this process are likely to set examples of how to achieve economic transformation and prosperity on the continent. This may be particularly important in that some suggest that state-building has been particularly challenging in Africa. The challenge may have consequences for the paths of economic transformation in Africa; it also suggests that African transformation might differ from experiences in other regions of the world.

An understanding of what constitutes good governance and whether institutional dualism—the tension between new institutions intended to enhance performance and unwanted old practices—damages core functions of government is essential to determine whether "good" governance is a limitation to development (Brinkerhoff and Goldsmith 2005). But African countries are believed to have been handicapped in several ways in generating institutions and governance that support rapid economic transformation. In precolonial times, Africa was characterized by traditional societies with limited bureaucracy and formalized rule of law (Goody 1971). Colonialists often created "artificial" states and established highly centralized governance systems,

---

[1] The ongoing global economic crisis has also affected economic performance in Africa. The food and fuel crisis led to increasing inflation and to current account and government deficits for 2008 in many countries. The financial crisis and the associated global recession are likely to hit financial inflows, such as foreign direct investment (FDI), remittances, and grants, while the African banking system is likely to be largely unaffected by the crisis due to its low exposure. However, in this research monograph we take a medium- to long-term perspective and assume that the global economy will resurge in the coming years.

which have often subsequently been inherited or adopted by African elites after their countries achieved independence (Young 1994). This centralized structure, combined with a lack of qualified personnel, has often led to the failure of postindependence governments in effectively allocating public investments and providing services, a situation aggravated by the great heterogeneity of preferences among various ethnic groups in the new nations (Pearson 1969; Alesina and La Ferrara 2005). In addition, the reliance on minerals and export revenues from a few agricultural products in many countries has resulted in a narrow tax base and high volatility of state revenues that have often favored corruption and nepotism among ruling governments (Gelb et al. 1988; Auty 1990). Although all of these may limit or retard development on the continent, it is useful to remember that the concept of a "soft state" was developed to characterize the lack of ability of corrupt states in Asia, which have ultimately managed to overcome those limitations to achieve considerable transformation (Djurfeldt et al. 2005). Countries such as Indonesia, Laos, and the Philippines are multiethnic and have precolonial formations and stateless societies within their borders as do some of the African countries (Djurfeldt et al. 2005).

Ghana, a country that has made significant efforts to build institutions and state capacity, is a prime candidate to champion economic transformation in Africa. It has made rapid progress in state- and institution-building, and economic growth has accelerated in recent years. Ghana has become a stable democratic state, as demonstrated by a peaceful transition of power in two consecutive free and fair elections in 2000 and 2008. Governance indicators have been steadily improving, and in 2007 Ghana ranked ahead of the regional averages of Latin America, Asia, and Africa in most important governance indicators, including government effectiveness, regulatory quality, and control of corruption (Kaufmann, Kraay, and Mastruzzi 2008). The country is ranked among the top 10 African countries in terms of freedom of the press and academic freedom (Freedom House 2009). Its financial market development has made remarkable progress over the past years, including improvements in the banking sector, increasing trade volumes on the stock exchange, and the launch of government bonds (Yartei 2006; IMF 2008). The domestic tax base has been broadened significantly, marking an important step toward reducing the dependence on cocoa for government revenues. Decentralization has improved the allocation of public resources and the provision of services to address regional disparities (World Bank 2007b). Perhaps most important, Ghanaians are determined to reach middle-income-country status and catch up with successful transformation countries in Asia such as Korea, Malaysia, and Thailand, all of which started out at lower per capita income levels in the early 1960s than did Ghana in 2005.

Two main conventional measures of economic transformation, capital accumulation and productivity growth, have also improved significantly over the past years in Ghana. Ghana has experienced two decades of sound and persistent annual growth of around 5 percent and belongs to a group of very few African countries with a record of positive per capita GDP growth in this period. Capital investment has risen to an average of 30 percent of GDP. Revenues from oil exploitation in the range of an additional 10–30 percent of the 2006 budget are likely to support a further increase in public investment in the medium term (IMF 2008; Osei 2008). Improvements in the domestic banking sector, advancements in indicators related to doing business, and a large Ghanaian expatriate community are likely to further attract private investments, which have been at a high level recently. Improvement in productivity has started to play a more important role in growth, as indicated by an average annual total factor productivity (TFP) growth rate of 1.6 percent between 2001 and 2006 (Bogetic et al. 2007; World Bank 2007b). Economic transformation has also been accompanied by the improvement of people's welfare, as measured by the reduction in poverty; the country is bound to become the first Sub-Saharan African country to achieve the first MDG of halving poverty before the target year, 2015 (Breisinger, Diao, and Thurlow 2009).

In spite of this success, several key challenges remain for Ghana and many other African countries to accelerate the transformation process. First, agriculture still dominates many African economies, contributing more than 30 percent of total GDP (35 percent in Ghana), and the urbanization process remains slow, with about two-thirds of the population still living in rural areas (60 percent in Ghana) (Diao et al. 2007). Agricultural output growth (and hence a large share of GDP) is not driven by productivity growth. The yields of most crops in many African countries are still far below their potentials, and the level of modern technology adoption in agricultural production and processing is still extremely low (Evenson and Gollin 2003; Johnson, Hazell, and Gulati 2003). Agriculture remains highly dependent on rainfall in Africa, but less than 2-5 percent of total crop area is irrigated (3 percent in Ghana), and less than 20 percent of the irrigation potential is used (FAO 1997). On the other hand, the potential for land expansion has been reaching its limits in many African countries, urging a rapid shift toward a Green Revolution type of productivity-led growth.

A second challenge is the high level of dependence on a few agricultural products and mineral resources for export, which continues to make the internal and external macroeconomic balances of many African countries vulnerable to international price volatility and external shocks. For example, cocoa and gold contribute about two-thirds to Ghana's export revenues

(Breisinger, Diao, and Thurlow 2009). Third, manufacturing's contribution to growth, measured as the sector's shares of GDP or exports, has declined in many African counties after the implementation of structural adjustment programs (SAPs) in the 1980s and as a consequence of the failed state-led industrialization pursued in the 1960s and 1970s (Breisinger and Diao 2008). Although manufacturing growth has accelerated in recent years, economic growth linkages often remain weak, especially between rural and urban areas and between manufacturing and agriculture (Diao et al. 2007). Finally, accelerating the process of transformation will require functioning markets, including the development of an effective and efficient service sector. Trade, transport, finance, and communication are all key elements to further improve market access and efficiency in Ghana (World Bank 2008). Addressing these challenges and creating incentives and opportunities for the private sector to drive growth in agriculture, manufacturing, and services requires strong policy support and massive public investments to create an enabling environment.

In light of these opportunities and challenges, the Government of Ghana has strongly committed itself to pursuing its new vision of achieving economic transformation. Ghana's Second Growth and Poverty Reduction Strategy (GPRS II) reemphasizes the need for a "rapid and radical transformation of the structure of Ghana's internal production and foreign trade" (Ghana, NDPC 2005, ii). The medium-term goal defined by GPRS II is to achieve MIC status by doubling the country's per capita income to $1,000 or more.[2] In addition, GPRS II places a new emphasis on the role of agriculture in economic transformation. This new momentum for agriculture is underlined by Ghana's commitment to the Comprehensive Africa Agriculture Development Programme (CAADP) of the New Partnership for Africa's Development (NEPAD).

Objectives of This Research Monograph

Against the broad background just discussed and in light of the commitments of the Government of Ghana and the unique development momentum in Ghana and other African countries, the objective of this research monograph is to provide new insights into prospective transformation paths of the Ghanaian economy. More specifically, the monograph addresses the following questions:

- What can Ghana learn from transformation theory and from other countries' successful transformation experiences?
- What does Ghana's own postindependence history suggest, and what changes have taken place to provide a basis for more effective transformation and design of development strategies?

---

[2] All dollar amounts in this monograph are in US$.

- Given Ghana's progress in institutional development and macroeconomic stability and its current socioeconomic structure, what are the country's broad options to achieve economic transformation through accelerated growth?
- What role will the agricultural sector play in Ghana's economic transformation? Is productivity-led agricultural growth (a Green Revolution) feasible, and what are its potential impacts?
- What are the implications of the factors mentioned in these questions for development strategies in Ghana?

By addressing these questions, this research monograph makes three major contributions to the existing literature on economic transformation:
1. It contributes to a critical development topic by combining lessons from 50 years of international economic transformation and from Ghana's history with quantitative modeling techniques to provide an assessment of alternative scenarios for the future.
2. It combines conventional measurements of economic transformation with the equality and poverty impacts of transformation.
3. It contributes to the economywide modeling literature by introducing structural diversity and spatial differences into the model framework.

Outline of the Monograph
This monograph is organized as follows. After the introduction in Chapter 1, Chapter 2 reviews the literature on economic transformation theory and combines this review with an analysis of transformation experiences from selected countries relevant to Ghana's future transformation between 1960 and 2005. Based on this review and analysis, we define productivity-led growth, rapid capital accumulation, intersector linkages, and institutions/markets as the main sources of economic transformation. Applying this framework to Ghana's postindependence history, Chapter 3 focuses on major lessons learned from the past and derives implications for future development strategies. The broad literature on Ghana's economic history and particularly a recent book that documents interviews with Ghanaian experts provide rich sources of knowledge for us to draw lessons from in this chapter. Chapter 4 turns to the recent performance of Ghana's economy by providing an overview of its current economic structure and discussing opportunities and challenges for future economic transformation. Special emphasis is given to potential drivers of economic growth at the sector level, thereby laying the foundation for the quantitative analysis that takes up the next two chapters. We develop a dynamic computable general equilibrium model for this analysis. Thus, Chapter 5 first introduces the modeling method, the data used, and the main limitations of the

model, which are followed by the scenarios designed for the modeling analysis. Chapter 6 discusses the model results of five selected scenarios in which the roles of different economic sectors in transformation, equality promotion, and poverty reduction are quantitatively measured and compared. Chapter 7 summarizes the principal findings of the monograph and discusses the implications for Ghana's development strategies.

CHAPTER 2

Lessons from Transformation Theory and Practice

Economic Transformation Reconsidered

Identifying the sources and processes underlying economic transformation has been an ongoing challenge for many generations of economists, as exemplified by Lewis's statement that "the economist's dream would be to have a single theory of growth that took an economy from the lowest level past the dividing line of $2,000 . . . and beyond" (Lewis 1984, 4). Despite the lack of this type of general theory, early development economists have approached this issue by defining several stylized facts that characterize the outcome of transformation processes. First, industrialization triggers a rapid increase in the share of manufacturing in the economy and a concomitant decline in agriculture's share (Chenery 1960; Kuznets 1966; Chenery and Taylor 1968). Second, the share of labor employed in the agricultural sector falls while that in other economic sectors rises. However, the absolute number of laborers employed in the agricultural sector often does not decline as quickly as the sector's share in GDP (Fisher 1939; Hayami and Ruttan 1985). Third, in this process the center of the country's economy shifts from rural areas to cities, and the degree of urbanization significantly increases (Kuznets 1966). The interrelated processes of these structural changes that accompany economic development are jointly referred to as economic transformation (Syrquin 1988).[1]

These stylized facts defined by early development economists are still applicable to the recent transformation stories, yet there are significant differences in the speed of structural change and economic growth between countries. To learn lessons from these experiences for Ghana's transformation, we select all countries that have reached middle-income status in the past four decades for further analysis. The country selection is based on the World Development Indicator database (World Bank 2007a, 2008) and uses the following three criteria: (1) the per capita income of each selected country

---

[1] We use this definition for economic transformation throughout the monograph.

Table 2.1 Economic structure of selected countries in transformation, 1960s–2005

Region, country	Initial year[a]	Share in GDP Agriculture	Share in GDP Manufacturing	Year reaching middle-income-country status	Share in GDP Agriculture	Share in GDP Manufacturing	Share in GDP, 2005 Agriculture	Share in GDP, 2005 Manufacturing
Latin America								
Brazil	1965	20.6	22.3	1975	12.1	26.1	8.1	22.0
Costa Rica	1965	29.4	18.4	1976	23.3	22.5	8.7	21.9
Dominican Republic	1965	23.2	15.6	1980	20.1	15.3	12.4	15.1
El Salvador	1960	41.4	15.6	1992	14.6	24.4	10.3	23.1
Mexico	1965	13.7	19.5	1974	12.0	22.8	3.8	17.7
Paraguay	1965	36.7	15.5	1989	29.6	14.5	22.1	12.4
Asia								
China	1982	33.3	37.3	2001	14.1	31.6	12.6	33.5
India	1978	38.9	16.6	2005	18.3	15.7	18.3	15.7
Indonesia	1974	31.1	9.2	1995	17.1	24.1	13.4	28.1
Malaysia	1960	34.3	8.1	1977	26.5	19.2	8.7	30.6
Philippines	1972	29.5	26.5	1995	21.6	23	14.3	23.3
Sri Lanka	1973	27.3	17.4	2005	16.8	14.9	16.8	14.9
Thailand	1972	25.3	18.4	1988	16.2	25.8	9.9	34.7
Vietnam	1994	27.4	14.9	2005	20.9	20.7	20.9	20.7
North Africa								
Egypt	1974	29.4	17.8	1996	17.3	17.7	14.9	16.8
Morocco	1965	23.4	15.7	1990	17.7	18.4	14.1	16.6
Tunisia	1965	20.8	8.1	1979	24.4	20.2	11.6	17.5

Source: Calculated using World Bank (2008).
Note: GDP means gross domestic product.
[a] A year when the country had a per capita income of US$400 or less or the first year that data were available.

was around or below $400 in the 1960s, comparable to that of Ghana in 2005; (2) the country became a MIC in the four decades since1962, reaching a per capita GDP of $1,000 or more;[2] and (3) the country is not classified as rich in mineral resources.[3] We focus on the period in which a country has moved from a low income level to MIC status and use this period as an approximation of the transformation. This makes the analysis relevant to Ghana, because the initial stage of each of the selected countries is consistent with Ghana's current situation, and the end stage of each in the period is consistent with the country's development objectives as defined in GPRS II.

Surprisingly, only 17 countries meet our selection criteria and qualify for further investigation. Among these countries, 6 are in Latin America, 8 in Asia, and the remaining 3 in North Africa. We focus on 15 of these countries, excluding two small countries (Guyana and Swaziland) due to their small populations of fewer than 2 million. We also include India and Vietnam in the analysis. Although these two countries have not yet reached MIC status, their rapid growth indicates their potential to do so within the next few years. Thus their economic development can provide important additional information for this study. The analysis of these 17 countries focuses on their economic structural changes, urbanization, and growth acceleration.

Structural Change

Table 2.1 first describes the economic structure of each of the 17 countries at three points in time: (1) the initial year, defined as when the country had a per capita income of around $400; (2) the year when the country reached MIC status; and (3) 2005, the latest year for which consistent data were available. As shown in Table 2.1, in spite of the heterogeneity of the countries, rapid growth was accompanied by significant structural changes in all countries. Although the initial volume of agriculture in the economy varied (in a range of 21–41 percent of the countries' GDP), there was no single country in which agriculture constituted more than 30 percent of GDP when its per capita income reached more than $1,000, regardless of the country's size. Except for Malaysia and Paraguay, at the time when each of the selected countries reached the MIC level, the share of agriculture in its economy fell to between 12 and 24 percent of GDP and further fell to 8–22 percent in 2005 (including in Malaysia and Paraguay).[4] The sharpest decline of agricultural shares

---

[2] According to World Bank classification (World Bank 2008).

[3] Some countries are not included due to the lack of data. We also exclude mineral-rich countries, because many of them have become MICs without significant transformation.

[4] Mexico is an exception, because its share of agriculture was low in 1965 (13.7 percent). This share fell further, to 3.8 percent in 2005.

occurred among the Asian countries, and this decline was mainly due to the more rapid expansion of manufacturing and services than agriculture (which will be further discussed later). There were two countries, Malaysia and Paraguay, in which agriculture still accounted for 26.5 percent and 29.6 percent of the respective economies when their per capita incomes surpassed $1,000 (see Table 2.1). There were also four other countries in which the share of agricultural was still higher than 20 percent in the year when each country reached MIC status. These findings suggest that Ghana may follow a similar path toward a lower agricultural contribution to overall economic growth. However, given that the current agricultural share in Ghana's economy remains as high as 35 percent of GDP, understanding the role of agriculture in the country's transformation, as in many other African countries with similar initial conditions, will be critical.

The declining role of agriculture in the economy implies that industry and services have become more important for economic growth. Within industry, manufacturing has been a main driver of transformation in many countries during their early development processes. Comparing initial manufacturing shares in the study countries shows that manufacturing as a share of GDP is substantially higher in most cases than Ghana's 10 percent in 2005 (see Table 2.1). Four out of the 17 selected countries had a manufacturing share of GDP higher than 20 percent in the early stage of transformation, while the shares of the other 10 countries ranged between 14.9 and 18.4 percent. In only three of the selected countries did manufacturing initially account for less than Ghana's level in 2005. Indonesia and Malaysia provide two interesting cases, with comparable manufacturing shares to Ghana and high agricultural shares at the time these two countries started their transformation. On the way to MIC status, Indonesia raised its manufacturing share from 9 percent in 1974 to 24 percent in 1995, while Malaysia more than doubled its manufacturing share (from 8 to 19 percent) within 17 years. These findings underline the important role of manufacturing-led growth for transformation in Ghana. Even in countries with large agricultural sectors, manufacturing constituted an important part of the transformation story.

In India, the service sector has been an important driver of growth on the way to MIC status. The share of the service sector in India increased from 36.6 percent in 1978 to 54 percent in 2005, while the share of manufacturing declined (World Bank 2008). Growth in services was primarily driven by the export-oriented information technology sector and supported by the availability of skilled labor. Yet in most low-income countries such as Ghana, services are mainly nontraded, and service-sector growth typically depends on growth in other sectors. Although cross-country comparisons of service-sector growth are complicated by the diversity of the sector's structure, including public and private, traded and nontraded, high and low value added, knowledge-intensive and unskilled labor–intensive,[5] the Indian example demonstrates that an export-oriented, service-led growth strategy is a viable transformation option, one we will further explore for Ghana in Chapter 5.

Demographic Transformation

Table 2.2 illustrates structural change in terms of urbanization by using the share of rural population as a proxy. As in Table 2.1, the changes in the shares of the rural population are given at three points in time. The majority of the population in most study countries (except Mexico) lived in rural areas at income levels comparable to those of Ghana. The share of the rural population ranged between 50 and 80 percent of the total population in the initial year and has been generally much higher in the Asian countries compared to the countries in other regions. The rural share of the total population fell significantly around the time the countries became MICs. Yet in 15 of the 17 countries, more than or close to 50 percent of the population still lived in rural areas when their per capita income reached $1,000. Although only Brazil and Mexico had become "urbanized economies" in 2005 (with rural shares of their total populations below 25 percent), 11 of the studied countries retained a rural share of more than 40 percent, and in some Asian countries even around 60 percent of the population still lived in rural areas (China, India, Sri Lanka, Thailand, and Vietnam).

It is important to note that a decline in the rural population share does not necessarily correlate with a decline in the absolute number of rural people. Among the 17 selected countries, Brazil presents the only case in which the rural population in 2005 was smaller in absolute numbers compared to 1960. Five more countries experienced negative rural population growth between 1990 and 2005; among them, four were Asian countries, namely China, Indonesia, Malaysia, and the Philippines. In the remaining 11 countries, the rural population consistently increased in absolute terms throughout the transformation period. In 11 of the selected 17 countries, 40 percent or more of the population still lives in rural areas today. These results indicate that urbanization is a much slower process than change in economic structure. They also suggest that despite the increasing importance of urban areas, a significant number of people will continue to reside in rural areas in Ghana for many years into the future. Given the important role of agriculture in rural economies, agricultural growth continues to play an important role in releas-

---

[5] Therefore, we do not herein examine changes in the service sectors of the selected economies during transformation.

Table 2.2   Urbanization: Share of the rural population in selected countries during transformation, 1960s–2005

Region, country	Year	Share	Year	Share	Share in 2005
Latin America					
Brazil	1960	55.1	1975	38.3	15.8
Costa Rica	1960	65.7	1976	58.3	38.3
Dominican Republic	1960	69.8	1980	48.7	33.2
El Salvador	1960	61.7	1992	48.9	40.2
Mexico	1960	49.2	1974	38.0	24.0
Paraguay	1965	63.8	1989	52.0	41.5
Asia					
China	1982	79.0	2001	63.3	59.6
India	1978	77.6	2005	71.3	71.3
Indonesia	1974	81.1	1995	64.4	51.9
Malaysia	1960	73.4	1977	60.6	32.7
Philippines	1972	66.0	1995	46.0	37.3
Sri Lanka	1973	80.5	2005	84.9	84.9
Thailand	1972	77.9	1988	71.1	67.7
Vietnam	1994	78.2	2005	73.6	73.6
North Africa					
Egypt	1970	57.8	1996	57.3	57.2
Morocco	1963	69.1	1990	51.6	41.3
Tunisia	1961	62.1	1979	60.6	32.7

Source: Calculated using World Bank (2009). Initial years might vary from those in Table 2.1
        due to availability of data.
Note: India and Vietnam had not yet reached middle-income-country status by 2005.

ing the pressure on migration and urban–rural income distribution in the growth process.

In addition to rural–urban shifts, demographic transformation is also characterized by a shift to lower levels of mortality and fertility and thus by changing dependency rates (Box 2.1). Table 2.3 shows that child mortality in the selected countries fell from between 59 and 226 per 1,000 children in the initial years of transformation to between 29 and 109 at the time of reaching MIC status. The initial levels were lowest in China, Sri Lanka, and Vietnam, while the sharpest declines during the transformation period were observed in Egypt, El Salvador, Sri Lanka, and Thailand. Fertility rates also fell sharply in all countries, most notably in India, Indonesia, Sri Lanka, and Thailand. At the time of reaching MIC status, fertility rates in these countries were down to 1.9–2.7 percent and were the lowest rates among all selected countries (except China).

These changes matter for economic transformation, because demographic transition can contribute to economic growth if the working-age population grows at a much faster pace than the dependent population (Bloom and

---

Box 2.1   Demographic change

Ghana is passing through a demographic transition, and the reduction in its population growth will translate into a decreasing dependency ratio. In Ghana, the working-age population currently represents just over half the population and is increasing (from 52 percent in 1983 to 57 percent in 2005). The number of young people (the 0-14 age cohort) has decreased from 45 percent to 39 percent, and the proportion of people over age 65 has increased slightly but remains low, at 4 percent. Because the proportion of people who are too young or too old to work is falling and there are more working people relative to dependents, the economy could benefit from this (potential) drop in the dependency ratio. Population projections show that in 2025 Ghana will reach zero population growth, which will translate into a decreasing dependency ratio. To benefit from this decreasing dependency ratio, however, the economy must create sufficient jobs and both the existing active population and the new cohort who enter the labor force need to find work.

Source: Adapted from World Bank (2007b).

Williamson 1998). Our descriptive analysis shows that the dependency ratio fell by double digits in all cases (except in Mexico), indicating that changes in the ratio of dependents (children) to the working-age population might have contributed to growth acceleration during transformation. However, for this demographic effect to accelerate growth and transformation, supportive social, economic, and political institutions have to be in place.

Periods of Growth Acceleration

Although the recent transformation experiences are consistent with the stylized facts identified by the early development economists, we find that structural changes have also been accompanied by periods of rapid growth acceleration in most countries. Table 2.4 reports average growth in GDP and agricultural GDP for the selected 17 countries. We pay particular attention to that subperiod in the transformation process in which growth accelerated. In general, the average level of growth over the entire period of 45 years was high in most countries. As shown in Table 2.4, the average annual growth rate between 1961 and 2005 ranged between 5.0 and 8.6 percent in 8 of the 17 examined countries and between 3.6 and 4.6 percent in another 8 countries. In only one country, El Salvador, was there a relatively low growth rate. In

Table 2.3   Changes in rates of child mortality, fertility, and dependency during transformation, 1960s to middle-income-country (MIC) status

Region, country	Initial year[a]	Child mortality[b]	Fertility[c]	Dependency[d]	Year reaching MIC status	Child mortality	Fertility	Dependency
Latin America								
Brazil	1965	157.3	5.7	82.7	1975	109.0	4.5	72.2
Costa Rica	1965	104.0	6.4	95.2	1976	55.0	3.8	74.2
Dominican Republic	1965	141.5	6.9	99.1	1980	88.1	4.3	78.8
El Salvador	1960	191.0	6.7	88.0	1992	60.0	3.7	71.8
Mexico	1965	122.1	6.8	94.4	1974	95.1	5.9	92.8
Paraguay	1965	83.5	6.3	96.8	1989	41.3	4.5	76.1
Asia								
China	1982	58.9	2.3	54.2	2001	36.6	1.7	36.8
India	1978	156.2	4.9	69.5	2005	76.9	2.7	53.1
Indonesia	1974	153.0	5.0	76.6	1995	66.0	2.7	52.7
Malaysia	1960	113.0	6.8	88.2	1977	55.0	4.2	73.7
Philippines	1972	89.0	6.0	86.0	1995	44.4	3.9	68.8
Sri Lanka	1973	69.0	4.1	65.8	2005	21.0	1.9	35.9
Thailand	1972	102.6	5.1	83.1	1988	31.0	2.3	49.3
Vietnam	1994	73.6	2.8	66.2	2005	39.9	2.2	45.1
North Africa								
Egypt	1974	208.6	5.7	78.2	1996	71.7	3.5	69.6
Morocco	1965	197.0	7.1	90.7	1990	93.2	4.0	70.6
Tunisia	1965	226.0	7.0	92.4	1979	100.0	5.2	78.4

Source: Authors' calculations based on World Bank (2008).
Note: When information for a specific year was not available, we chose the value of the closest year.
[a]A year when the country had a per capita income of US$400 or less or the first year that data were available.
[b]Under 5 years, per 1,000 children.
[c]Total births per woman.
[d]Under 15 years to working age.

general, Asian economies (except for the Philippines) grew faster than the countries outside Asia, and the growth rates in Latin American and African countries were relatively modest. Driven mainly by rapid Asian growth, the 17 selected countries as a group grew by 5.5 percent annually (or 5.1 percent without country weights) over the 45-year time frame. This growth rate is significantly higher than that of the world economy on average (1.7 percent) and that of the low-middle-income group as a whole (3.6 percent) over the same period of time.[6]

The high growth rate in the transforming countries was the outcome of growth acceleration in at least one subperiod and sustained growth after that. All 17 countries experienced one distinct period with rapid growth during which growth averaged between 7.0 and 9.8 percent for the 8 fastest transformers and between 5.0 and 6.7 percent for the other 9 countries (see Table 2.4). Periods of accelerated growth began either in the 1960s, as in the case of the 6 Latin American countries and some countries in the other regions, or in the early 1970s, as in many Asian countries (excluding China).[7] These growth periods ended in the early 1980s in all 6 Latin American countries, 3 African countries, and 2 Asian countries. Moreover, most of the selected countries managed to sustain growth over a relatively long period of time; relatively rapid growth lasted from 15 to 37 years in 14 countries and between 11 and 14 years in the remaining 3 countries. Although some of these countries experienced relatively slow or even negative growth in some years, this slowdown rarely lasted for more than one year, and growth acceleration continued after that in most cases. To measure the growth fluctuation, we calculate the coefficient of variation (CV) using the actual annual growth rate. The CV value confirms relatively stable growth for most of the countries during their growth acceleration periods. The CV value is less than 0.5 for 14 countries; that is, the standard deviation of the actual annual growth rate in absolute terms is less than 50 percent of the absolute value of the average annual growth rate for these countries and between 0.56 and 0.66 for the remaining 3 countries in Latin America and Africa.

Agricultural growth rates are generally lower than growth rates for the overall economy, yet the agricultural sector expanded by more than 4 percent annually for a period of 10 or more years in 10 of the 17 countries (5 in Asia). Relatively rapid agricultural growth in the early years seems to support overall growth acceleration in Asian countries (see Table 2.4). However, many of the Asian countries experienced agricultural growth deceleration in later

---

[6] Only El Salvador and the Philippines have an overall growth rate of 3.6 percent or below.

[7] Growth acceleration actually started in the 1950s in the Latin American countries, but there are no consistent data available for this period.

Table 2.4   Growth performance of selected countries in transformation (add average AgGDP growth rate for 1961–2005)

Region, country	Average annual growth rate, 1961-2005	Period	GDP growth acceleration		AgGDP growth acceleration	
			Annual growth rate	Number of years	Annual growth rate	Number of years
Latin America						
Brazil	4.4	1965-81	7.8	20	4.0	16
Costa Rica	4.6	1965-75	6.6	17	6.9	10
Dominican Republic	5.0	1966-83	7.2	17	5.2	18
El Salvador	2.2	1967-79	5.0	18	3.5	13
Mexico	4.1	1965-81	6.6	21	3.1	21
Paraguay	4.6	1965-81	7.7	15	5.2	21
Asia						
China	8.6	1978-96	9.8	28	5.1	19
India	4.7	1988-2005	6.1	15	2.8	17
Indonesia	6.2	1968-89	7.1	30	4.0	22
Malaysia	6.8	1965-89	7.0	37	4.0	18
Philippines	3.6	1965-80	5.3	11	3.8	16
Sri Lanka	4.6	1973-85	5.3	13	3.8	13
Thailand	6.9	1965-85	7.6	36	4.6	24
Vietnam	7.2	1988-2005	7.4	18	4.1	18
North Africa						
Egypt	5.4	1969-90	6.7	16	2.9	21
Morocco	4.1	1965-76	5.9	14	3.3	10
Tunisia	5.1	1965-81	6.5	19	5.7	20

Source: Calculated using World Bank (2008).
Notes: India and Vietnam had not yet reached middle-income-country status by 2005. Due to a lack of early 1960s-era agricultural data for many countries, we are unable to calculate the AgGDP growth rate for the period 1965-2005. Therefore, we use the 1960-2005 period for the GDP growth calculations. AgGDP means agricultural GDP; GDP means gross domestic product.

years concurrent with continued expansion of their economies.[8] With the exceptions of China and Paraguay, no country experienced an average annual agricultural growth rate of more than 4 percent over the 45-year period (1961–2005) compared to 15 countries with total annual GDP growth rates of more than 4 percent. Yet, as in the case of the average GDP growth rate, the average annual agricultural GDP growth rate for the study group (3.8 percent) was

[8] The lack of early 1960s-era data on agricultural growth in the Latin American and African countries prevents us from analyzing the relationship between agricultural growth acceleration and economic growth in these countries. However, it appears that the same factors noted earlier as causing overall economic collapse, or external shocks such as oil price surges, were also likely to be responsible for the agricultural growth slowdowns in the Latin American and African countries.

still remarkably higher than the 2.1 percent average annual growth rate of world agriculture or the growth rate of the MICs as a whole (2.8 percent).

This relatively shorter period of agricultural growth can be explained by the high volatility of agricultural growth. In stark contrast to overall GDP growth, the CV value for the actual annual agricultural growth rate of 1965–2005 is higher than 1 for most countries, as high as 11.2 for Morocco, and between 2.2 and 3.7 for three other countries, Costa Rica, the Dominican Republic, and Tunisia. Compared with the CV value for GDP growth, only China's agricultural growth was slightly less volatile than its overall economic growth, while for seven other countries (Costa Rica, India, Malaysia, Morocco, Sri Lanka, Thailand, and Tunisia), agricultural growth was 3–10 times more volatile than overall economic growth.

The foregoing analysis suggests that rapid and sustained growth is necessary for Ghana and other African countries to successfully pursue transformation. The other countries' experiences also indicate that although periods of growth slowdown and volatility have often occurred, these periods have to be very short for the transformation process to be sustained. The analysis of agricultural growth experiences suggests that sustaining agricultural growth is more challenging mainly due to the sector's inherent high volatility, caused by weather shocks. This growth volatility in Africa's (including Ghana's) agriculture is relatively great due to its high level of dependency on rainfall and international markets. Thus, managing volatility is a challenge for Ghana to support rapid and sustainable agricultural growth and thus make agriculture an important contributor to the process of transformation in the country.

Income Distribution and Poverty

Early transformation theory focused on growth and structural change and paid less attention to changes in income distribution. An important contribution to this issue was made by Kuznets (1955), who argued that income inequality might follow an inverse U-shaped relationship during the development process, implying that industrialization leads to an initial increase in inequality, followed by a decline in inequality as the process continues. However, empirical evidence of the validity of this prediction remains weak, and inequality has actually increased in many developed countries over recent decades (World Bank 2008). These increases in inequality have become increasingly important issues in the transformation process, even in successfully transforming countries such as China and Thailand. Experiences from Latin America and other regions suggest that neglecting this issue at early stages of transformation can create persisting long-term development challenges (Breisinger and Diao 2008). Therefore, enhancing the participation of the poor in the transformation process through public investments in physical and human capital and linking the poor to the transformation process through different income transfer schemes have widely been accepted as important parts of transformation strategy and policies in order to minimize the negative impacts of uneven development and to avoid entrenched sharp divisions in society (Coady, Grosh and Hoddinott 2004; Timmer 2008).

Addressing inequality and poverty dimensions in the transformation process, however, remains a challenge for both analysts and practitioners. For analysts, the difficulty concerns the availability of information on the measures of inequality and poverty. Consistent data are available only for recent years, yet most study countries reached MIC status in the 1980s. Second, because of the stark differences between countries and the complexity of comparing inequality and poverty across countries, most studies are country specific, and generalizations from these studies are difficult.[9] However, the literature identifies several factors that contributed to the increases in inequality during the transformation process. In general, the initital conditions in the distribution of assets matters. The distribution of assets (particularly land in rural areas) and incomes has varied significantly across the 17 selected countries, and increases in inequality have often related to the early stage of asset distribution. For example, high Gini coefficients (and high levels of inequality in the distribution of assets) have characterized many Latin American countries (such as Brazil and Mexico) even at the beginning of the transformation process, and inequality has subsequently increased in both countries. On the other side, income disparities can also increase in countries that start the transformation process with a relatively more equal distribution of assets. While Vietnam's Gini coefficient remained relatively stable and changed only slightly, from 0.36 in 1993 to 0.37 in 2004, China's Gini coefficient, initially similar to that of Vietnam, increased to an estimated 0.47 in 2004 (World Bank 2008). Contrary to these experiences, Gini coefficients in Thailand have actually decreased, from 0.49 in 1993 to 0.42 in 2004 (World Bank 2008).

Poverty reduction trends are also markedly different among countries. Although China and Vietnam have seen dramatic reduction in poverty, periods of stagnant growth in several countries, starting in the early 1980s, have led to increases in absolute poverty, particularly in the rural areas. In fact, the recent national poverty rates were reportedly as high as 50 percent in the Dominican Republic and Paraguay (World Bank 2008), a poverty rate comparable to or even higher than that in many low-income countries.

---

[9] Cross-country analysis is also complicated by a lack of consistent time-series data on incomes and poverty.

The trade-offs and long-term costs to development of increasing inequality and persistent poverty are still not well understood. Modern development economists have therefore suggested complementing measures of successful development with social and environmental indicators. Amartya Sen has championed such a more multidimensional approach by looking beyond the level of income, defining human "well-being" as an indicator for measuring development outcomes (Sen 1998). A practical application of Sen's approach is the Human Development Index, which has been compiled by the United Nations since 1990 (UNDP 2009).[10]

The important message for countries like Ghana that are embarking on the process of transformation is that the increase in inequality has the potential to slow down the development process and that persistent poverty embodies a significant challenge for the future. Positive examples of shared growth, such as those of Thailand and Vietnam, have emphasized growth in sectors where the majority of the poor earn their living, whereas countries with persistent poverty traps and large income disparities have often neglected agriculture in the transformation process (Breisinger and Diao 2008).

Institutions and Markets

Institutional change in general and market development in particular are necessary parts of transformation. As stated by Matthews (1986), the choice of technique or institution may affect both institutional change and market development, albeit in opposite directions. Most economists agree that the quality of institutions can explain differences in growth and transformation processes by shaping incentives to develop new technologies and innovation (Easterly and Levine 2003; Rodrik, Subramanian, and Trebbi 2004). Moreover, by drawing lessons from studies in several countries, Rodrik finds that the onset of the transformation process does not necessarily require extensive institutional reform; rather, institutional reform should be seen as an endogenous part of the transformation process (Rodrik 2003).

Technology-led productivity change involves the intensive use of modern inputs purchased from markets. The availability of seasonal financing, more developed marketing systems, and supply chains built around smallholder farmers becomes increasingly important in agricultural transformation, requiring simultaneous and complementary investments in all links of the supply chain. However, lack of coordination, opportunism, rent-seeking costs, and risk can all complicate the effectiveness and efficiency of such simultane-

---

[10] Due to the relative novelty of the Human Development Index, in this monograph we can make only limited use of this indicator to examine changes during economic transformation.

ous investments (Poulton, Kydd, and Dorward 2006). The lack of market institution development and investment in infrastructure and information systems results in high transportation and transaction costs, forcing farmers to remain within a traditional subsistence mode of production. Moreover, increased use of modern inputs and growing agricultural production can significantly increase the market and profitability risk of small farmers in the process of transformation, further decreasing their incentive to adopt new technology.

The active role of the state in transformation during the 1950s and 1960s was based on the optimistic view that transformation or development in general can be accelerated by a defined series of policies and direct public interventions. The pre–World War II economic crisis, the existence of market underdevelopment, and the pervasiveness of market failure in developing countries forced many governments to engage in central planning. Additionally, the apparent initial success of central planning in many Eastern Bloc countries further encouraged governments to rely on the "commanding heights" of the state rather than the market (Yergin and Stanislaw 1998). The core elements of this strategy included planned investment in capital accumulation, use of rural surplus labor reserves, adoption of import substitution industrialization (ISI) strategies, and a series of policy interventions in international trade and domestic markets.

To finance state-led industrial development, governments often discriminated against agriculture and other export-oriented sectors. Overvalued exchange rates, high import duties on intermediates and capital goods, and heavy taxation of agricultural exports all undermined the role of sectors that would otherwise have had comparative advantages in leading growth and structural change (Krueger, Schiff, and Valdes 1991). Within agriculture, the most important state interventions from the 1960s to the 1980s were the direct involvements of governments in market activities. Input and output marketing and processing facilities in many developing countries (especially in Africa) were almost always operated by semiautonomous government or parastatal agencies or by mostly government-initiated cooperatives on a monopoly basis. However, the operations of most public marketing agencies tended to be costly and inefficient because of overstaffing and inexperienced management. In addition, small-scale private trading, often in informal, traditional markets, was discouraged. According to *World Development Report 2008* (World Bank 2007c), public expenditure reviews suggest that in many countries a large share of public spending in agriculture has been allocated to providing private goods at high costs, even in recent years.

Direct government interventions aimed at correcting market failures frequently resulted in extensive "government failures,"[11] which inhibited positive market responses and development. Although market failure is often the result of inappropriate incentives rather than a lack of responsiveness (Krueger 1986), 20 years after the inception of the World Bank / International Monetary Fund (IMF) SAPs, which sought to correct prices and markets, underdeveloped markets are still a predominant phenomenon in many African countries, particularly for staple commodities that are produced mostly by small farmers. However, in many other developing countries, especially successfully transforming countries, a great deal of progress has been made, primarily led by the private sector. In Africa, inadequate transport infrastructures and services in rural areas continue to push up marketing costs and undermine local markets and export opportunities.

More recent analysis suggests that African governments have removed their earlier antiagriculture and antitrade policy biases; the average rates of taxation of agriculture are now below those of the 1960s (Anderson and Masters 2007). In Ghana, for example, the distortions that affected the agricultural sector prior to 1983–84 have since been removed for the most part. A few distortions remain, however. The Ghana Cocoa Board has increased its share of export earnings since the 1990s, and rice and maize are still protected (Brooks, Croppenstedt, and Aggrey-Fynn 2007).

The reason for inadequate development of markets or institutions is contentious. Some argue that the role of the states has not been rolled back adequately to facilitate private-sector development, while others argue that the reforms may have gone too far. Jayne et al. (2002) argue that most fundamental aspects of reform were not implemented, were reversed, or were implemented in such a way that the private sector could not develop to replace the state institutions; that some wrongly diagnose the reason for the lack of private-sector response as underinvestment in public goods, overlooking the policy barriers; and that market reform is not quick but ought to be a continuous process of searching for alternative institutional arrangements. Friis-Hansen (2000), on the other hand, arguing that reforms may have gone too far, notes several concerns: that reforms may have been implemented without adequate concern for country differences, and the context in which the liberalization was implemented has made countries worse off; that the private sector has not filled the gap, and in many cases it is not profitable for the private sector to provide services that were previously subsidized to

---

[11] Government failure is the public-sector analogue to market failure.

various degrees; that structural adjustments may have favored the better-off farmers, leaving those in the peripheral areas more vulnerable; and that public institutions whose roles have changed have not managed to fulfill their new roles effectively.

In addition to focusing on the state as the institution to address market failures, we must recognize that there is a "third sector" that can play an important role in remedying market failures. This third sector comprises producer organizations, nongovernmental organizations (NGOs), and other civil-society groups (World Bank 2007c). Farmer-based organizations can facilitate economies of scale for inputs such as fertilizers, seeds, and extension and for the marketing of outputs. These organizations can also play an important role in the management of resources and joint infrastructure, such as watersheds and irrigation systems (World Bank 2007c). NGOs often have a comparative advantage in local networking and knowledge. These competencies of NGOs and others can be harnessed for improving local service delivery and standard setting, for example, the fair trade labeling of products (World Bank 2007c). Finally, especially in countries like Ghana with relatively high levels of political freedom and information sharing, civil-society groups can play an important role in giving political voice to smallholders, rural women, and agricultural laborers and in holding policymakers accountable for their promises and political actions (World Bank 2007c).

With more liberalized markets, the public sector still needs to have a role in technology development, especially for agricultural transformation. The national or international transfer of agricultural technology involves the adaptation of location-specific technology to different environmental conditions (Hayami 1974). This means that public institutions must conduct adaptive research whereby agricultural experiment stations promote research outcomes and improve the capabilities of regional farming populations. Public spending on such research should also be combined with conventional public investments in roads, transportation, and irrigation facilities, which together form the most important and successful government interventions in an early Green Revolution. Today public investments in rural infrastructure—including irrigation, roads, transport, power, telecommunications, market development, rural finance, and research—are considered the most important factors for long-term agricultural development (World Bank 2007c).

Recent studies also emphasize the importance of the efficiency and sequencing of public investments in agriculture. Economic outcomes are often unsatisfactory, and many public resources are wasted when public spending and policies are biased toward large-scale production and the state sector. This sector often constitutes a small share of total production, and such policies ignore the majority of smallholders (as seen in many African countries during the late 1960s and the 1970s). For example, large-scale state farms throughout Africa absorbed substantial public resources from the 1960s to the 1980s (Meier 1989). Furthermore, the resources spent on agricultural input and other subsidies have often been used inefficiently and ineffectively. In Zambia, for example, until very recently about 80 percent of the nonwage agricultural budget was spent on agricultural subsidies, whereas spending on research, extension services, and rural infrastructure (that is, investments that have shown high payoffs) accounted for only 15 percent of this budget (World Bank 2007c). The efficiency of public investment is also constrained by institutional capacity. For example, there is no doubt about the importance of irrigation to the success of the Green Revolutions in Asia and Latin America, but an important factor in this success was the existence of a relatively complex institutional capacity, along with the management experience necessary to efficiently operate irrigation systems. Institutional capacity and its important role in transformation is discussed further later.

A great deal of work remains to be done to improve the performance of marketing systems in developing countries. The existence of both market failures and government failures calls for a better understanding of the interaction between the public and private sectors and the role of institutions in transformation. Such an understanding is often country specific, and the path to the successful transformation of institutions in general and to market development in particular often requires experimentation, a willingness to depart from orthodoxy, and attention to local conditions (Rodrik 2003). However, recent market developments under globalization and the rapidly growing local and international demand for agricultural products have opened up important new opportunities for developing countries to find their paths to transformation through the joint efforts of the private and public sectors.

Sources of Transformation

The previous sections of this chapter have mainly focused on the *outcomes* of economic transformation. The remainder of the chapter focuses on the *sources* of transformation, which can be grouped into four categories: productivity changes, capital accumulation, strengthening of linkages, and improvements of institutions/markets. Following this classification, we summarize the relevant economic theory in the context of the transformation experiences of the 17 study countries. Due to the important role of agriculture in transformation, we further examine agriculture as a source of transformation.

Productivity-Led Growth

Productivity growth led by innovation and technology adoption is a "permissive" source of transformation and a necessary condition for development

(Kuznets 1973, 247). The educational levels of society, or the human capital, play an important role in innovation and adoption.[12] In addition, there is evidence that human capital enhances productivity spillovers from foreign direct investment and increases the returns to other factors (World Bank 2005a). For example, educated farmers are more likely to adopt new technologies such as improved seeds and fertilizer and thus consistently have higher returns from their land (Jimenez 1995).[13]

Experiences from our sample of countries confirm the importance of productivity-led growth. Productivity increased in all the countries except El Salvador and the Philippines between 1960 and 1990 (Nehru and Dhareshwar 1994).[14] The annual TFP growth rates varied from 2.2 percent in China and 1.7 percent in Thailand to around 1.5 in the three North African countries (see Appendix B). In contrast, the TFP growth rates in Africa were mostly negative during the same period, including in Ghana, with a negative growth rate of -1.2 percent.

Lewis's dual economy theory was the first seminal contribution to explaining how productivity growth leads to economic transformation (Lewis 1954). Observations on the streets of Bangkok inspired Lewis to hypothesize about the existence of a large traditional sector in which "the marginal productivity of labor is negligible, zero or even negative" in many low-income developing countries (Lewis 1954, 140; Lewis 1979). The difference between a leading modern sector (often the industrial sector) with higher productivity and a lagging traditional sector (often the agricultural sector) with lower productivity, combined with an unlimited supply of labor from this traditional sector (which keeps economywide wages down), allows production to grow in the economy through the migration of labor from the traditional sector to the modern sector. Led by productivity growth in the modern sector, this dual economy eventually converges to a single economy with equalization in the

---

[12] According to *World Development Report 2007* (World Bank 2006, 28), *human capital* refers to "a broad range of knowledge, skills, and capabilities that people need for life and work." In addition to this traditional notion, the *World Development Report* highlights skills and capabilities required for successful living: "These fall under three main categories: jobs, family, and community. Under jobs are a range of skills and capabilities required to obtain and retain a job above and beyond the technical competence to do the job, such as self-discipline and teamwork. Under family are health and such skills as good parenting and managing or resolving conflict. Under community are the skills and capabilities involved in belonging to a community, enjoying its privileges and protections, and living up to its obligations" (World Bank 2006, 28).
[13] Consistent data on education, such as number of students trained by primary/secondary/ tertiary level or educational levels of the workforce, are available only from the 1990s on.
[14] Consistent data for the periods of rapid transformation identified in the previous section are not available.

economywide marginal productivity of labor and full employment. Fei and Ranis further extended (or improved) the dual economy theory and pointed out the possible negative implications of agriculture's role in economywide growth within this model (Fei and Ranis 1961). They argued that if the withdrawal of labor causes food supplies to decline or the marginal productivity of labor in agriculture to rise to levels that are equal to the marginal productivity in the modern sector, growth in agriculture can either constrain or contribute to the growth of the modern sector.

The idea that productivity-led agricultural transformation can play an active role in transformation has been first promoted by Schultz (Schultz 1964, 1968). According to Schultz's "efficient but poor" hypothesis, providing farmers with incentives to adopt modern technologies can make agriculture an important driver of growth. Jorgenson also emphasized the role of agricultural productivity growth, stating that "unless technological progress in agriculture is sufficiently rapid to outpace the growth of population and the force of diminishing returns in land and other factors, the industrial sector may not become economically viable" (Jorgenson 1961, 311). In a similar vein, Kuznets argued that because agricultural growth is greater during periods of transformation than before transformation, industrial revolution is always accompanied by an agricultural revolution (Kuznets 1966). Tiffin and Irz (2006) go one step further and find that agriculture has been the engine of growth in most developing countries; that is, causality runs from agricultural growth to economywide growth in most cases. Irz and Roe (2005) show that even small variations in agricultural productivity have had strong implications for the rate and pattern of economywide growth.

The Green Revolution not only reinforced the view that technology-led productivity growth can transform traditional agriculture into a modern sector but also showed that agriculture helps accelerate the economywide transformation process. Evidence suggests that the rapid agricultural growth in many Asian and Latin American countries in the 1960s and 1970s was driven by the adoption of new farming technologies, including the use of irrigation, high-yield crop varieties, and modern inputs such as fertilizer. Agricultural productivity data from the 17 study countries support the active role of agriculture in transformation. Agricultural productivity has increased in most countries except for Paraguay and Sri Lanka, and growth has often been greater during initial years of transformation than over the long term (Table 2.5).

Rapid Capital Accumulation

Technology-led productivity growth is typically accompanied by rapid capital accumulation, because most technologies are embodied in modern capital goods. Capital deepening in the economy and in agriculture has been observed

Table 2.5   Agricultural productivity growth of selected countries, 1961-2006

Region, country	Period reaching middle-income-country status	Percent annual change	Entire period	Percent annual change
Latin America				
Brazil	1965-81	0.0	1961-2006	0.9
Costa Rica	1965-75	4.1	1961-2006	3.1
Dominican Republic	1966-83	2.0	1961-2006	1.1
El Salvador	1967-79	1.2	1961-2006	0.8
Mexico	1965-81	1.5	1961-2006	1.7
Paraguay	1965-81	-0.3	1961-2006	-1.8
Asia				
China	1978-96	0.7	1961-2006	-0.7
India	1988-2005	0.7	1961-2006	-0.2
Indonesia	1968-89	1.4	1961-2006	1.3
Malaysia	1965-89	0.7	1961-2006	1.0
Philippines	1965-80	2.8	1961-2006	0.7
Sri Lanka	1973-85	-0.7	1961-2006	-0.6
Thailand	1965-85	0.7	1961-2006	0.4
Vietnam	1988-2005	0.7	1961-2006	1.2
North Africa				
Egypt	1969-90	0.1	1961-2006	1.6
Morocco	1965-76	0.0	1961-2006	0.0
Tunisia	1965-81	0.0	1961-2006	0.0

Source: Nin-Pratt and Yu (2010).

in all successfully transformed countries (Chenery 1960; Kuznets 1961; Syrquin and Chenery 1986). In our sample of countries, for example, in the Asian countries, the investment share of GDP consistently rose from between 18.7 and 33.6 percent initially to between 23.4 and 37.3 percent when the countries reached MIC status. In the Latin American countries the investment share reached between 17.7 and 30.7 percent, and in North African countries it reached between 28.3 and 29.6 percent at the time that these countries reached MIC status (UN 2009).[15]

To finance investments, particularly public investments, governments have often treated the agricultural sector as a surplus provider for industrialization, consistent with Lewis's dual economy model. This was the rationale often used by developmental planners in introducing agricultural export taxes, high tariff protection in industry, and other measures (for example, overvalued exchange rates) aimed at transferring resources from agriculture

---

[15] Consistent data for the initial years are not available for Latin America and the North African countries.

to industry (Krueger, Schiff, and Valdes 1991). The bias against agriculture has decreased in Africa in recent years, and capital for investments has increasingly come from other sources, such as domestic savings, foreign direct investment (FDI), and loans (Anderson et al. 2008).[16]

FDI can play an important role during transformation, both directly through an increase in capital investment and indirectly through spillover effects. FDI inflows increased in most study countries during periods of rapid transformation, most notably in Brazil and China (Table 2.6). However, as a share of GDP, FDI inflows often remained below 2 percent, indicating the important role of domestic savings as the major source of investment. This suggests that the indirect effects of positive externalities, including technological spillovers, human capital formation from learning by doing, and the crowding-in of domestic investments associated with FDI, play a more important role than the direct effects of increased capital availability (Markusen and Venables 1999; Torvik 2001).

Economic Interlinkages

Productivity growth, capital accumulation, and changes in consumer demand enhance economic interlinkages during the transformation process.[17] Hirschman (1958) was among the first development theorists to emphasize the backward and forward linkages created by capital investments in the industrial sector. Johnston and Mellor (1961) thereafter extended this concept by emphasizing the importance of interactions between agricultural and nonagricultural sectors, especially in low-income countries. Many studies since then have shown that agricultural linkages in particular foster growth and employment, especially in low-income countries. Therefore, the nature of agricultural and nonagricultural linkages is likely to determine the course of transformation (Diao et al. 2007; World Bank 2007c).

Enhancing agricultural linkages with other sectors is embodied in the process of transforming traditional agriculture into a modern sector. This process strengthens both consumption and production linkages between agriculture and nonagriculture and between rural and urban areas. Backward linkages increase the demand for modern inputs such as fertilizer (produced by the manufacturing sector) and for marketing and trade (provided by the service

---

[16] High rates of investment shares of GDP are a necessary condition for rapid transformation, but the allocation of public and private investments also matters, and improving the efficiency of investments remains a major challenge to support successful transformation. Chapter 3 will discuss these issues in detail for Ghana.

[17] Changes in consumer demand mainly include the empirical observation that consumers shift their consumption patterns from food to higher-value consumer goods when incomes rise (Engel's Law).

Table 2.6   Role of foreign direct investment (FDI) in selected countries

Region, country	Initial year[a]	FDI[b]	Year reaching middle-income-country status	FDI[b]	Annual FDI growth[c]
Latin America					
Brazil	1965	0.9	1975	1.1	32.8
Costa Rica	1965	2.7	1976	2.6	21.4
Dominican Republic	1965	4.8	1980	1.4	-1.2
El Salvador	1960	0.3	1992	0.3	4.6
Mexico	1965	0.9	1974	0.7	14.7
Paraguay	1965	0.6	1989	0.3	-4.7
Asia					
China	1982	0.0	2001	3.3	29.9
India	1978	0.0	2005	0.8	26.3
Indonesia	1974	0.7	1995	2.2	10.5
Malaysia	1960	2.2	1977	2.9	29.2
Philippines	1972	0.1	1995	2.0	24.3
Sri Lanka	1973	0.0	2005	1.1	31.4
Thailand	1972	0.8	1988	1.8	13.7
Vietnam	1994	11.9	2005	3.7	6.8
North Africa					
Egypt	1974	0.0	1996	0.9	42.9
Morocco	1965	0.5	1990	0.2	26.8
Tunisia	1965	1.1	1979	0.7	18.0

Source: Authors' calculations based on World Bank (2009).
[a]A year when the country had a per capita income of US$400 or less or the first year that data were available.
[b]Foreign direct investment, net inflows (percentage of gross domestic product).
[c]Annual growth of FDI inflows during transformation (initial year through the year reaching middle-income-country status).

sectors). In addition, consumption linkages lead to large growth multipliers and poverty reduction effects, especially in low-income countries with large agricultural sectors (Delgado et al. 1998; Christiaensen, Demery, and Kuhl 2006; Diao et al. 2007; World Bank 2007c). Forward linkages ensure the supply of agricultural raw materials for processing industries. A stagnant agricultural sector is therefore likely to inhibit industrial and service-sector growth due to a lack of rural purchasing power growth and a lack of input supply. Growth in agricultural productivity and output, on the other hand, ensures the provision of food at low prices, as well as cheap raw materials for various industries (for example, food processing), thereby opening up opportunities for the development and diversification of food manufacturing and marketing activities.

The existence of these linkages between a modern agricultural sector and the rest of the economy also poses several transformation challenges. In the case of Ghana, modern inputs used in agricultural production are not produced locally. The increased use of fertilizer, therefore, might put an additional burden on the external balance, depending on its use and its marginal returns. In addition, modern inputs (for example, improved seeds) are often location specific, with the consequence that imported varieties are of limited use in increasing productivity. Instead, local research institutions must find ways to adapt modern seeds to local conditions and develop new forms that are appropriate to Ghana's diverse agroecological condition. Finally, the supply of modern factors within a country also depends on factors and activities outside of agriculture. Hence, transforming agriculture in Ghana, as elsewhere, will require increased efficiency and modernization across the whole economy (Hayami and Ruttan 1985).

Lessons for Ghana from Successfully Transforming Countries

The stylized facts characterizing the process of economic transformation remain meaningful indicators of successful transformation. Productivity-led growth, capital investments, and strong linkages, markets, and institutions are still the key to this success. Six major lessons emerge from these transformation experiences for Ghana:

1. Transformation is characterized by rapid economic growth, which generally raises the income levels of the poorest population groups. However, the persistence of poverty and increasing income inequality in many transformed economies exposes the limitations of welfare measures based solely on per capita income. Rapidly increasing inequalities call for a broader definition of the transformation process and the incorporation of wider-ranging goals for development. However, income divergence was pronounced during the growth collapses or slowdowns in many Latin American and African countries, indicating the importance of constant and sustained growth.

2. With this new understanding of transformation, the next important message is that the role of agriculture in transformation seems to be even more important today than it was four decades ago. Although Schultz and other agricultural and general economists have recognized the important contribution of agricultural transformation to the development process, today we see that this contribution is also perfectly consistent with the role of agriculture in shared growth and the reduction of poverty and inequality. Bypassing small farmers during the process of agricultural modernization marginalizes a large segment of the rural population and is likely to lead to social tensions. It also complicates long-term poverty reduction and improvements in income inequality, even after the country as a whole reaches middle-income status.

3. Productivity growth led by the adoption of modern technology is key to economywide and agricultural transformation. Smallholder farmers are entrepreneurs and became vanguards in the adoption of new technologies and in increasing agricultural productivity during the Green Revolution in many Asian countries. However, smallholders face many external constraints that cannot be overcome by their own strengths, and therefore they need supportive government policies and public investments. The most important policy action must be the removal of urban- and industry-biased policies regarding trade, marketing, taxes, and other macroeconomic factors. The most important public investment must be in rural infrastructure, including irrigation, and the provision of agricultural research and extension to a majority of farmers.

4. Growth in manufacturing and services must be led by the private sector and supported by government policies and public investments. Improving the physical and institutional environment is critical to providing incentives for the private sector to do business and create competition. Winner-picking industrialization strategies and related policies may help create a large industrial sector, but this sector often fails to establish close links with the rest of the economy. Moreover, the creation of this sector comes at high direct and indirect costs, especially with regard to agricultural transformation. Increased inequality and difficulties in making these "picked" industrial sectors internationally competitive and capable of generating sustainable long-term economic growth have taught painful lessons about this type of transformation strategy.

5. Private-sector-led manufacturing- and service-sector growth, which is more "homegrown" in nature, is likely to be more consistent with a country's initial condition and its comparative advantage in exports; hence, it can lead to broad-based growth. This type of transformation was seen in Thailand in the 1960s and 1970s and in China in the 1980s, during the early periods of sustained rapid growth in these countries. Moreover, this industrialization path is often more labor intensive and usually creates strong linkages with the rest of the economy, particularly with agriculture, by using agricultural materials as inputs. In fact, manufacturing often develops in rural areas in the form of rural nonfarm activities, and the creation of rural manufacturing has often played an important role in poverty reduction and rural transformation.

6. FDI can play an important role during transformation, both directly through an increase in capital investments and indirectly through spillover effects. The direct effect seems to be rather small in the early stages of transformation, and the indirect effects of positive externalities, including

technological spillovers, human capital formation from learning by doing, and the crowding-in of domestic investments associated with FDI, seem to play a more important role than do the direct effects of increased capital availability.

Using these general findings on the process of transformation, the next chapter will draw specific lessons from Ghana's country-specific experience.

CHAPTER 3

Lessons from Ghana's Economic History

Review of the outcomes and sources of transformation suggests that the pathways through which these forces shape transformation differ across countries. This diversity is often the consequence of the interactions among initial conditions such as a country's social, political, and institutional arrangements; the initial economic structure; and the policies and strategies implemented during the transformation process. Therefore, economists are increasingly promoting a country-specific approach in the quest to better understand development and identify growth opportunities and constraints on prosperity (Rodrik 2003). This approach focuses on the dynamics of development, where "history matters, change is central, structures are endogenous, and learning is at the heart of the story" (Stern, Dethier, and Rogers 2005, 86).

A rich body of literature exists on postindependence economic development in Africa, including many studies on Ghana, the country that first gained independence in 1957. For an overview of events, see Box 3.1. It may be unrealistic to draw selected conclusions from a synthesis of this broad literature given its wealth of information and diversity of focus, as well as the sometimes conflicting opinions derived from these reviews. Understanding that no consensus has been reached on the lessons and experiences of Ghana's postindependent development process, we focus our review on the factors that are likely to become more important for Ghana's future economic transformation. We tremendously benefited from a recent book, *An Economic History of Ghana: Reflections on a Half-Century of Challenges and Progress* (Agyeman-Duah 2008), in which the editors documents their interviews with 20 distinguished experts on Ghana's economy, politics, and society. Many of the contributors are Ghanaians and have personally witnessed or participated in the country's development process as scholars or officials. Notwithstanding the celebratory spirit of the document and the somewhat partisan assessment by some of the contributors of the role of the past two democratic regimes that have governed the country, the collection of essays does provide a balanced assessment of the situation and of changes that have occurred in the

Box 3.1   A short preindependence economic history (1880-1957)

The foundation of Ghana's economic structure was laid in the late 19th and early 20th centuries. This structure has shaped the country's development path for more than a century and will likely continue to play an important role in future growth and transformation. Although small-scale local gold mining, the export of palm oil and rubber, and local production of consumer goods (food, textiles, etc.) characterized the Ghanaian economy before 1880, the period between 1880 and 1914 saw a rapid expansion of cocoa, gold, and timber production (Green 1987; Berry 1993). The land area under cocoa expanded rapidly, and exports rose from 13 tons in 1895 to 5,093 tons in 1905 and reached a volume of 50,000 tons by 1914 (Hill 1997). European investments in mines and transportation infrastructure permitted rapid growth of exports of gold and timber (McLaughlin and Owusu-Ansah 1995). In addition to shaping Ghana's export structure, this period also marked the beginning of high import intensity in Ghana's economy. The newly established infrastructure and trade links led to the displacement of many locally produced goods with imports from Europe.

After World War I, the colonial government stepped up the use of export revenues for investments in economic and social infrastructure, including railways, a deep sea harbor, water supply systems, schools, hospitals, communication, and electricity (Berry 1993). These new investments supported the acceleration of export-led growth until the Great Depression, which caused a sharp fall in global commodity prices and halted or reversed growth in Ghana. Severe limitations on shipping and trade during World War II explain why growth did not return to the country until the late 1940s. Rising international commodity prices after the war stimulated the resurgence of Ghana's traditional exports and led to a renewed expansion of production, especially of timber and cocoa. By the end of the 1940s, Ghana had become the world's largest cocoa exporter, supplying more than half of the world's cocoa, and also a major exporter of timber and gold. By the time Ghana achieved independence in 1957, a process of peaceful political transition and one of the best infrastructure and education systems in Africa suggested good prospects for the country's economic development and transformation.

country. Many lessons discussed in this chapter are drawn directly from this book. We first focus on the lessons regarding the development visions and strategies of the postindependence period, then move on to the roles of institutions, policies, and policy implementation through which the visions and strategies have (or have not) been achieved.

The President's Development Vision Succeeded, though His Strategies Failed

As the first African country that gained independence, Ghana was seen as the hope and example for the whole continent. Although many criticize the policies pursued by Dr. Kwame Nkrumah, Ghana's first president, his vision to unite the country and build a modern industrialized country is widely recognized. Measured by per capita income, Ghana was at a development level similar to those of Indonesia, Malaysia, South Korea, and Thailand after they achieved independence in the late 1950s and early 1960s. Moreover, Ghana was rich in foreign exchange reserves due to its global dominance in cocoa exports (and exports of gold). With these initial conditions, the leadership of Ghana deeply believed in a modernization strategy that was led by the state, a strategy that was commonly accepted by almost all developing countries at the time. Until the late 1980s, the dominating role of the state in transformation was also almost unquestioned by the governments following Nkrumah, many of which took power through a series of coups d'états.

After five decades of postindependence experience and asked to draw lessons from this development period (which extended until the late 1980s), few question Nkrumah's vision for Ghana to become a modern developed country. Yet many also agree that the state-led modernization strategy failed and that it was indeed infeasible for Ghana given its initial conditions. The failure of this strategy to create a modern industrial sector in Ghana (as in many other countries) has made people realize that although modernization needs huge capital investments to create the physical foundation for a modern industrial sector, modernization goes beyond capital accumulation. Many contributors to *An Economic History of Ghana* also agree that the strategy of stabilization and privatization in the 1980s and early 1990s improved macroeconomic stability but without complementary measures failed to spark broader modernization.

Modernization is a process of development in which a country develops its social, institutional, human, and physical capacity to manage (not only by the public sector) and operate (mainly by the private sector) its growing economy. The term *modernization* is often used as a synonym for *transformation* by Ghanaian policymakers and scholars, which is why we adopt the term throughout this chapter. In this process, the state must play an important role, but this role is often constrained both by its capacity and by the relationship between the state and the private sector. Against this broad background and the key lessons learned from the past failure of the state-led approach in Ghana, we present some specific lessons drawn from the literature on the design and implementation of development strategies.

Political, Institutional, and Macroeconomic Instability Delayed Modernization

The frequent changes of governments in Ghana, many of which came to power by means of military coups d'états—although this experience is not very different from that of many other countries in postindependence Africa—damaged Ghana considerably by preventing it from moving from the inappropriate strategies that were adopted immediately after independence. However, in the past two decades, Ghana has been able to overcome the political, institutional, and macroeconomic instabilities that impeded its development.

The state-led approach to modernization adopted immediately after independence undermined Ghana's macroeconomic stability. It contributed to a rapid increase in macroeconomic imbalances and a vicious circle of policies inimical to modernization. Massive public investments in infrastructure, health, education, and state-owned enterprises (SOEs) under the Nkrumah government had quickly gone beyond the capacity of the state to generate revenues from the narrow base of export sectors. Moreover, the capital-intensive investment strategy exacerbated the need for additional capital and foreign exchange. Because neither domestic savings nor foreign capital (through either FDI or foreign loans and grants) was sufficiently available to support this capital-intensive development strategy, the government resorted to introducing import tariffs and printing currency, resulting in an increase in inflation and increased costs for imported inputs. To avoid further raising the costs of imports, the exchange rate was held at highly overvalued levels. To generate more domestic capital, the government established new banks and raised taxes. Efforts to correct the negative employment effects of these mechanisms led to strong interventions in the labor market. In addition, the government actively generated employment by expanding the public sector, which resulted in a 250 percent increase in publicly paid employees between 1957 and 1966. Subsequent governments failed to correct these imbalances despite several "traditional" adjustment measures, including the devaluation of the currency, liberalization of trade, balancing of the budget, and attempts to privatize SOEs.

State-Led Development Policies Continued through Various Regimes Despite Their Rhetoric

A change in the development path of state-led modernization was complicated by the frequency and disruptiveness of government changes until 1992 (see the chronology in Appendix C). The two governments following the Nkrumah administration (1967-72) attempted to reverse some of Nkrumah's ISI policies and intended to implement a more market-oriented and private-sector-driven approach. However, their industrialization strategy continued to be biased in favor of capital-intensive sectors, and the attempts at privatizing SOEs largely failed. In the agricultural sector, a shift of focus from large-scale agriculture toward smallholders was also short lived and ineffective. The administration of Ignatius Kutu Acheampong (1972-78) refocused on national self-sufficiency to address the accelerating economic decline and the rise in poverty. There were then two more presidents and one military coup before the government under Lieutenant Jerry Rawlings decided to adopt an Economic Recovery Program (ERP) and shift away from state-led development.[1] Political stability under democratic governance was finally restored by a new constitution in 1992, the year in which Rawlings was elected president in the first free and fair election since 1960.

Political Instability Also Eroded Institutional Memory and Capacity in the Civil Service

Ghana's political instability and discontinuity also weakened and politicized its civil service. Ghana's first president, Nkrumah, inherited a capable civil service on independence. Nkrumah's perception that the civil service was not loyal to him led him to Africanize the service by placing Ghanaians in leadership positions (Cato 2008). The frequent change in governments thereafter often went hand in hand with changes in top civil service positions. These frequent changes in staff eroded the civil service from "custodians of institutional memory" (Chinery-Hesse 2008, 36) to an often demoralized staff with deteriorating skills. They also cultivated a climate in which loyalty to specific governments became more important than competence and the assignment of civil service positions became a way to reward political supporters. This produced a class of opportunistic policy advisers who feared that their "wings would be clipped" (Cato 2008, 25), as well as civil servants with deteriorating skills. Finally, this politicization of the civil service has exacerbated the disruption created by transfers of power by holding back documents, files, and information from one government to the other.

---

[1] The ERP was Ghana's version of a SAP under the IMF and the World Bank.

Macroeconomic Stability Alone Has Not Been Enough to Accelerate Modernization

The ERP initiated in 1983 marked the first comprehensive attempt to achieve macroeconomic stabilization and to increase the role of the private sector in transformation. The ERP was Ghana's version of an IMF / World Bank SAP and started with a series of macroeconomic stabilization measures. The exchange rate was adjusted from a highly overvalued rate of 2.75 cedi per $1 in 1982 to 36.97 cedi per $1 in 1984 (IMF 2008). The increasing cost of imports was partly offset by the abolition or reduction of import taxes, from an average level of 40 percent to 10 percent (Leechor 1994). The elimination of subsidies combined with a tax reform based on a broadening of the tax base restored fiscal discipline and led to a small budget surplus in 1986. Inflation came down from more than 100 percent in 1983 to levels of around 30 percent in the following years (IMF 2008). However, a lack of commitment by the government to fully implement the ERP (Omtzigt 2008) and its one-sided focus on correcting price discrepancies and improving price incentives limited the impacts of the ERP on modernization (see the following sections on agriculture and industrialization). The country has failed to attract FDI in manufacturing; the response to the efforts of the government to improve the investment code and strengthen property rights has been limited, particularly in manufacturing, which is central to Ghanaian desire to transform the economy (Aryeetey 2008).

Ghana's Development Goals Have Often Been Too Ambitious

Ghana Has Often Been Impatient and Set Ambitious Development Goals That It Has Failed to Aggressively Pursue

The approach of the various governments has not been consistent. Governments in Ghana have often been too ambitious and unfocused in pursuing their goals, and there has often been a "rush to claim success" (Aryeetey 2008, 86). For example, Nkrumah's government converted a 10-year plan inherited from the colonial government into a 5-year plan with the consequence of rapid depletion of reserves and massive accumulation of public debt. It is also argued that Ghana tried to industrialize prematurely and pursued this course for several decades unsuccessfully. Sir Arthur Lewis was the first to advise the government to be more patient with industrialization in his report to the government in 1953. Along the line of his dual economy theory, Lewis argued that due to the country's land abundance labor was too expensive, and unless surplus labor was available, industrialization was not feasible. The conditions for industrialization may be more appropriate now that the price of labor has significantly decreased and the situation is closer to those that enabled East Asian economies to industrialize.

Ghana Has Often Not Set Realistic Development Goals Adapted to Local Conditions

The development of realistic policies also requires knowledge of local conditions. Yet many governments in Africa (including Ghana) have not done their "homework" by understanding and analyzing the country's situation before designing their strategies (Aryeetey 2008, 82). In many cases, governments have simply implemented policies that have proved successful in other countries or used policies proposed by outsiders as a blueprint for development without taking their own judgment and the country's local conditions sufficiently into account. Although there is debate as to how much choice governments had, given the conditionalities attached to the SAP loans, it is widely accepted that the development of the capacity and culture to design and implement policies owned by the country and the ability to negotiate with donors on an equal intellectual level is critical for success. But a comprehensive approach to developing strategies is now taking root in Ghana (Aryeetey 2008). Economic management of the country in general has improved (Akoto-Osei 2008).

The Earlier Strategies Did Not Seek Broad-Based Agricultural Development

Agricultural Development in the Immediate Postindependence Era Narrowly Focused on Foreign Exchange Earnings from Cocoa and Public Investments in Large-Scale Farming

Revenues from cocoa exports were key to finance state-led industrialization and continued to play an important role in the government budget. However, the Cocoa Marketing Board, originally founded to administer the notoriously volatile world market prices, has often been used to extract unsustainably high taxes from cocoa farmers for the general government budget rather than for price stabilization. In addition, agricultural policies have often been biased against small-scale farmers and non-cocoa export agriculture. Public investments and policies favored the creation of state-owned farms and cooperatives, and subsidies for agricultural mechanization, services, and inputs explicitly targeted large-scale farms. Overvalued exchange rates reduced the competitiveness of export agriculture and thereby discouraged agricultural export diversification.

Piecemeal Approaches to Agricultural Development Offered Limited Benefits

The first government with an explicit focus on agriculture and rural development was that of Kofi Abref Busia (1969-72), which shifted away from the focus on cocoa and large farms by investing in rural infrastructure such as roads, electrification, and rural water. In an attempt to focus more on small-scale agriculture, agricultural SOEs were dismantled and their machinery and equipment sold to private farmers. However, the failure to link these programs to an increase in agricultural productivity rendered them largely ineffective. In addition, these policies were short lived, and instead of continuing and complementing the agricultural policies of his predecessor with Green Revolution-type measures, Acheampong (1972-78) reversed much of the smallholder focus, reduced agricultural spending, and returned to large-scale production bias and mechanization under Operation Feed Yourself.[2]

Without a Comprehensive Long-Term Strategy and Public Investments, the Agriculture Sector Has Not Developed

The ERP increased producers' incentives to increase cocoa output through the devaluation of exchange rates and a reduction of export taxes. However, the lack of a comprehensive agricultural development and investment strategy limited the positive impacts on other agricultural sectors. Public investments remained low and tended to focus on single measures. For example, the Sasakawa Global 2000 project started in 1986 to promote integrated maize packages for small farmers. It reversed the earlier mechanization strategy by promoting animal traction as a substitute for tractors and also by providing technological transfer, farm inputs, and credit. Another example is the cocoa sector rehabilitation effort during the 1980s, which provided improved planting materials to many farmers and thus helped the sector respond to improved incentives during the reform period (Edwin and Masters 2005). Although these and other single measures such as cassava disease control and mechanization of rice production might have had localized impacts, they did not transform agriculture and bring about the Green Revolution type of growth seen in Asian countries. Major reasons for the limited success of these programs have been the unfinished privatization of input suppliers, poor infrastructure (especially storage and roads), and limited marketing opportunities for outputs.

---

[2] Spending on agriculture declined by about 26 percent per year despite the government's objective of reaching food self-sufficiency under the Operation Feed Yourself program.

The Private Sector Played an Important Role in Industrialization

State-Led Capital-Intensive Industrialization Did Not Work for Ghana

The absence of a strong private sector in Ghana has been used as an argument to modernize the economy on the backs of SOEs. However, the performance of these SOEs has often been disappointing, and hundreds of SOEs never managed to operate profitably or never even started operating at all. Although some efforts have been made to determine market demand with consumer surveys based on which factories have been built, there have been many examples of bad planning and implementation in the process. For example, a mango cannery was built that had a capacity to produce several times the world demand for canned mangoes (Omtzigt 2008). Despite these failures and the change in rhetoric that emphasized more market-oriented strategies in the 1970s, it was not until the 1990s that an intensive program of state divestiture of the SOEs got under way. Two of the few remnants of SOE development that are still operating today are the Akosombo hydropower dam and the VALCO aluminum smelter.

Experiences from Asian countries have shown that private-sector-led manufacturing and service-sector growth that is "homegrown" is likely to be more consistent with a country's initial conditions. Hence, homegrown manufacturing and service sectors take full advantage of the country's comparative advantage in the expansion process and are also likely to lead to broad-based growth (Breisinger and Diao 2008). This type of transformation has proved most important during the early period of transformation, as shown by Thailand's success during the 1960s and 1970s and China's rapid rise in the 1980s. This path to industrialization often requires less investment in physical capital, depends on local knowledge and "know-how," and more efficiently uses a country's abundant resources (for example, low-skilled labor). Moreover, this industrialization path usually quickly creates strong linkages with the rest of the economy, including agriculture, by enhancing mutual demand for such things as agricultural products as inputs (to enhance market-oriented activities) and mutual supply of these things. In fact, in the early stage of industrialization, small manufacturing factories/shops have often first operated in rural areas as rural nonfarm activities. With rising market demand these small entities often grow in scale, and then, with the addition of international expertise and capital, can become leading export sectors (Breisinger and Diao 2008). Ghana's comparative advantage in low-skilled labor favors a similar development path. In addition, failed state-led attempts to "create" large-scale industries around consumer goods such as tomatoes, juices, bottles, and textiles strongly suggest that the private sector has to take the lead in manufacturing and service-sector development.

The Public Sector Has to Play an Active Role in Providing Incentives for Modernization

The ERP begun in 1983 focused on macroeconomic stability and indirect measures to attract private capital for industrial development. Reestablishing fiscal stability required a reduction and reallocation of the government budgets and hence development strategies focused on indirect measures to stimulate growth. Priority in public investment allocation was given to the transportation, communication, and electrification sectors. In addition, new regulations such as those facilitating the repatriation of profits, tax breaks on intermediate inputs, and so on, attempted to attract capital for investments. These measures were most successful in the mining sector (gold), an enclave sector with few linkages and employment opportunities, yet failed to spark private investments in manufacturing. In addition, and despite the improvement of the macroeconomic environment and institutions, Ghana has not attracted significant amounts of FDI in manufacturing, a major "source of worry" (Aryeetey 2008, 77).

In light of these past challenges, there are signs of new opportunities for accelerating transformation in Ghana. The next chapter will discuss these opportunities and potential constraints in detail.

CHAPTER 4

Economic Structure and Future Outlook: Opportunities for and Constraints on Accelerating Transformation

The previous chapter highlighted how political and macroeconomic instability, a narrow-based agricultural strategy, and state-led industrialization delayed economic transformation in Ghana until the 1980s. However, in a sharp break with the country's past, sustained growth and significant poverty reduction since the early 1990s has made Ghana an African success story. Many factors have contributed to this impressive performance, including improvements in policies and the investment climate, increases in both private and public investments, increased foreign aid and remittance inflows, and favorable world prices for cocoa and other export commodities (McKay and Aryeetey 2004; Bogetic et al. 2007). The 2005–06 Ghana Living Standards Survey (GLSS5) suggests that, based on current trends, the country will reach the first MDG, halving its 1990s poverty rate, by 2008 (GSS 2007). Thus Ghana has become one of only a few African countries able to achieve MDG 1 earlier than the target year, 2015.[1] With this success in growth and poverty reduction, the Government of Ghana has declared its new development goal of reaching MIC status in the next 10-15 years, which will require that Ghana double its per capita GDP from the 2005 level of $454 to $1,000 over a period of 10-15 years.

Against this background, this chapter takes a forward-looking approach and highlights major opportunities for and challenges of accelerating Ghana's growth. This chapter also provides the base from which we conduct a quantitative assessment of future transformation paths in Ghana in the following two chapters. In addition to providing general perspectives on the macroeconomic and institutional outlook, we specifically focus on major constraints on and opportunities for agriculture and manufacturing-led growth.

---

[1] These projections are based on the situation that existed before the global financial crisis. As mentioned in note 1 on page 1, in this monograph we assume that global economic growth will resume in the coming years.

Ghana's Current Economic Structure

In 2005 the agricultural sector was the largest contributor to GDP in Ghana, followed by services and industry (Table 4.1). Agriculture's share of total GDP is 35 percent but increases to more than 40 percent once agriculture-related manufacturing is included. Within the agricultural sector, root and tuber crops, including cassava, yams, and cocoyams, account for 24 percent of agricultural GDP. Export crops, such as cocoa, oil palm, fruits, vegetables, rubber, and cotton, account for 21.3 percent of agricultural GDP. Cereals account for 9.3 percent and other staple crops 22.7 percent, while the live-stock sector contributes 7.1 percent.

Industry accounts for 30.5 percent of Ghana's total GDP, and construction (not manufacturing) is the largest industrial subsector. Manufacturing accounts for 33 percent of industrial GDP, dominated by agriculture-related manufacturing of items such as food, processed wood, and textiles. Construction accounts for 34.5 percent of industrial GDP, and the sector's growth has been primarily driven by an urban housing boom and infrastructure developments. Mining is also an important industrial subsector, accounting for almost 22 percent of industrial GDP. The service sector is larger than the indus-

Table 4.1   Current economic structure in Ghana, by sector, 2007

Sector, subsector	GDP	Exports	Imports	GDP share in sector total
Agriculture	35.1	36.3	7.3	100.0
Cereals	3.3	—	4.5	9.3
Root crops	8.4	—	—	23.9
Other staples	8.0	—	0.1	22.7
Export crops	7.5	25.2	—	21.3
Livestock	2.5	—	2.7	7.1
Fishery and forestry	5.5	11.1	—	15.5
Industry	30.5	41.7	87.8	100.0
Mining	6.7	—	—	22.0
Construction	10.5	—	—	34.5
Agriculture-related manufacturing	6.4	—	—	21.1
Other manufacturing	3.7	—	—	12.0
Other industry	3.2	—	—	10.4
Services	34.4	22.0	4.9	100.0
Private	22.7	22.0	4.9	65.9
Export-oriented	0.7	—	—	2.1
Public	11.0	—	—	32.0
Total	100.0	100.0	100.0	

Source: Breisinger, Thurlow, and Duncan (2007).
Notes: — indicates that there were no imports or exports of this product. GDP means gross domestic product.

trial sector; however, about one-third of the sector relates to government-provided services such as administration, health, and education. Private services include trade, transport, communication, hotel, restaurant, real estate, and business services. Some private services, such as those provided by luxury hotels and restaurants (mainly providing services to foreigners), are export oriented, yet those services account for only a relatively small portion of private services.

Agricultural structure and the regional distribution of agricultural GDP significantly differ across Ghana's agroecological zones. These regional differences have important implications for subsector-level agricultural growth strategies, which will be explored further in Chapter 6. The Forest Zone remains the major agricultural producer, accounting for 43 percent of agricultural GDP compared to about 10 percent in the Coastal Zone and 26.5 and 20.5 percent in the Southern and Northern Savannah Zones, respectively (Breisinger et al. 2009). The Northern Savannah Zone is the main producer of cereals and livestock. More than 70 percent of the country's sorghum, millet, cowpeas, groundnuts, beef, and soybeans come from the Northern Zone, while the Forest Zone supplies a large share of higher-value products, such as cocoa and livestock (mainly commercial poultry). The heterogeneous agricultural production structure also indicates differences in the agricultural income structure across regions. The Forest Zone generates about half its agricultural income from two of Ghana's major types of export goods (cocoa and forestry goods). Including nontraditional exports and fishery, export agriculture also plays an important role in total agricultural income for the Coast and Southern Savannah Zones. In contrast, 90 percent of agricultural income in the Northern Savannah Zone comes from staple crops and livestock.

There are also regional disparities in terms of incomes and poverty. Steady, persistent, sector-balanced economic growth has also helped the country to significantly reduce poverty. Ghana's national poverty rate has fallen from 51.7 percent in 1991-92 and 39.5 percent in 1998-99 to 28.5 percent in 2005-06, a total decline of 23.3 percentage points over 14 years. More poverty reduction has been achieved in rural areas in both absolute and relative terms. The rural population accounts for more than 60 percent of the total population, and the rural poverty rate fell from 63.6 percent in 1991-92 to 39.2 percent in 2005-06, a decline of 24.4 percentage points. In the same period, the urban poverty rate decreased from 27.7 percent in 1991-92 to 10.8 percent to 2005-06, a decline of 16.9 percentage points. However, regional inequality significantly increased, mainly due to a more modest decline of poverty in the poorest Northern Savannah regions. The poverty rate remained as high as 62.7 in the north by 2005-06, while the poverty rate reached 20 percent in the rest of Ghana.

Prospects for Economic Transformation

General Prospects

All 20 contributors to Agyeman-Duah's book on the economic history of Ghana generally paint an optimistic picture of the country's future. On the macroeconomic front, the recent launch of Ghanaian government bonds in the London market has been a great success. The bonds were issued for $750 million and oversubscribed by $3 billion, a "mark of confidence" in the country's creditworthiness (Cato 2008, 31). The prospects for both private and public investments are also seen as promising: FDI is likely to increase due to improved political and economic stability as well as improvements in the business climate index and property rights. Ghana is no longer seen as a country "where investment may prosper under one regime at best, but could not be guaranteed under the next one" (Gyimah-Boadi 2008, 223). In addition, 3 million Ghanaian expatriates, or about 14 percent of the population, are likely to sustain the inflow of remittances in the future. Finally, the debt relief provided under the HIPC (Heavily Indebted Poor Countries) program in 2002 and the recent discovery of oil have improved the fiscal scope for public investments to support productivity-led economic transformation.[2]

Productivity-led growth plays an important role in transformation processes, and the prospect for such growth in Ghana might have improved due to better incentives for and access to new technologies. Growth accounting analysis shows that TFP has indeed become an increasingly important driver of growth and explains much of Ghana's recent economic growth. Before this recent increase in TFP, fixed capital accumulation was a major contributor to growth, indicating a certain time lag between capital accumulation and productivity growth (Table 4.2). However, there have been other reasons to explain the recent increase in TFP. Bogetic et al. (2007) estimate that 27-30 percent of this recent TFP growth came from inter- and intra-sector labor reallocation, while technology advances may have contributed less than 10 percent of total growth. Results from Nin-Pratt and Yu (2008) confirm the results of intersector shifts (Table 4.3). Due to an increase in agricultural TFP, labor has shifted out of agriculture and into other sectors, as predicted in Lewis's dual economy model.

Although innovations were often prevented by a system of political patronage in the past, improved political transparency, human capital, and the spread of information technology are likely to improve incentives for the

---

[2] The HIPC program was initiated in 1996 by the International Monetary Fund and the World Bank to provide debt relief and low-interest loans to cancel or reduce poor countries' external debt repayments to sustainable levels (IMF 2010).

Table 4.2   Growth decomposition in Ghana (percent), 1970-2005

Average annual growth rate of selected indicators	1970-2005	1991-95	1996-2000	2001-05
Average annual growth rate				
Real gross domestic product	2.7	4.0	4.2	5.2
Fixed capital accumulation	2.1	4.3	5.9	3.9
Labor force	2.7	2.8	2.3	2.5
School years of the labor force	0.8	0.8	0.9	1.0
Total factor productivity	-0.26	0.05	-0.07	1.60
Contribution to growth				
Fixed capital accumulation	31.6	43.7	56.2	29.8
Labor force	61.3	42.6	32.8	28.5
School years of the labor force	16.9	12.4	12.7	11.1
Total factor productivity	-9.9	1.3	-1.6	30.6
Total	100.0	100.0	100.0	100.0

Source: Bogetic et al. (2007).
Note: The share of capital (α) in the Cobb-Douglas production function is assumed to be 0.4, while the depreciation rate is 4 percent.

Table 4.3   Breakdown of agricultural total factor productivity (TFP) growth in Ghana (percent), 1961-2006

Agricultural TFP			
Period	1961-90	1991-99	2000-06
Annual growth rate	0.29	2.31	2.71
Agricultural workers			
Year	1990	2000	2006
Share in total workforce	68.98	64.06	63.46

Source: Nin-Pratt and Yu (2008).

private sector to lead growth. School enrollment rates have increased for primary and secondary schools, respectively. The net enrollment rate for primary schools in Ghana is 78.6 percent, compared to the African average of 66.3 percent. Nearly 93 percent of those completing primary school in 2005–06 continued to the next level (World Bank 2007b). In addition, expatriate Ghanaians are expected to play an increasingly important role in innovation, and many have already done so with "a confidence in the limitlessness of what one can achieve" (Ofori-Atta 2008, 234). For example, expatriate Ghanaians have been leading the setup of the Ghanaian stock exchange, and further improving economic prospects might attract more expats to follow this example and start businesses in their home country. Productivity-led growth is also likely to be supported by better economic management.

Institutional capacity-building over the past two decades has also improved the analytical and planning skills of the civil service, and there are encouraging signs of improved coordination among government agencies, such as the setup of the Economic Policy Coordination Committee (Akoto-Osei 2008). Given this generally positive outlook on institutional and macroeconomic matters, in the remainder of this chapter we focus on challenges for transformation of the real economy, particularly agriculture and manufacturing.

Manufacturing

The manufacturing sector has not yet become the driver of modernization in Ghana as it did in other successfully transforming countries. Although the industrial sector, including utilities and construction, constituted 30.5 percent of Ghana's GDP in 2007, the manufacturing sector's share in GDP has been less than 10 percent since the 1970s (see Table B.1). The sizes of both industry and manufacturing in Ghana's economy are comparable to those in Malaysia in 1965, and the size of Ghana's industry is also similar to that of Thailand in 1976, India in 1992, and Vietnam in 1997 (see Table 2.1). However, the share of manufacturing in those three countries' economies was much higher than that in Ghana's today. Ghana's manufacturing sector accounts for only 33 percent of industrial GDP and is dominated by activities heavily dependent on agricultural inputs, such as food and wood processing. Agriculture-related manufacturing accounts for 21 percent of the country's industrial GDP. Imports of industrial goods such as capital goods, oils, and chemical products (including fertilizer) cause a large trade deficit, equal to 12 percent of industrial GDP (see Tables B.2 and B.3).

There are several encouraging signs that manufacturing, especially "homegrown" manufacturing, can play an increasingly important role in Ghana's transformation. Although the transformation of traditional industries into modern sectors was often prevented by cultural reservations and lack of marketing skills in the past, further professionalization of entrepreneurs can harness the large potentials for traditional industries in Ghana (Oteng-Gyasi 2008). Entrepreneurs from Vietnam and China have shown how the adoption of modern production methods can transform traditional Ghanaian handicrafts into international businesses. Vietnamese entrepreneurs have successfully produced and marketed Bolga baskets (originally from northern Ghana) in Vietnam. Chinese entrepreneurs have revolutionized the market for kente cloth (used for the traditional Ghanian dress). Instead of using the traditional process for weaving kente cloth, the Chinese have started to imprint the textiles and thereby significantly lowered production costs.

Several initiatives also focus on the strengthening of linkages between manufacturing and the agricultural sector in the transformation process to add value to the country's rich agricultural resources (see Box 4.1 for more on such linkages). For example, under President John Kufuor's cocoa processing initiative, capacity use in two main processing companies, the Cocoa Processing Company and West African Mills Company, has been improved and new capacities have been either established or planned by two major international companies (Osei 2008). However, there is now concern that the local capacity may be constrained by an inadequate supply of cocoa, because the country may prefer to export beans of high quality that fetch a premium in global markets.

Agriculture

In Ghana agriculture accounts for 35 percent of GDP and 36 percent of export earnings and employs more than 60 percent of the labor force. Given the sector's initial size and its importance for incomes and foreign exchange earnings, agriculture is likely to play a key role in Ghana's economic transformation. The main driving force behind the rapid agricultural growth is the crop subsector (excluding cocoa), the largest subsector in agriculture, accounting for more than two-thirds of the agricultural economy (Table 4.4). Staple crops such as maize, sorghum, rice, cassava, yams, plantains, pulses, and oilseeds dominate this subsector. Some high-value crops such as vegetables and fruits are also included, but they play a relatively modest role in overall agricultural growth given their small size.

Cocoa is Ghana's most important traditional export crop and has received special attention from the government in terms of financial and policy supports. As a result of this attention, and with favorable world prices in recent years, the cocoa sector has grown most rapidly except for the period of 1996–2000 (see Table 4.4). Thus cocoa's contribution to agricultural growth is almost three times that expected from its size in the economy (see Table 4.4).

As in most African countries, agricultural growth in Ghana has been mainly driven by land expansion, and productivity-led growth remains a challenge. Table 4.5 shows that cultivated land has expanded by 60 percent over the past 12 years, from 4.5 million hectares in 1994 to 7.2 million hectares in 2006. Land expansion has slowed in recent years but has continued to expand at an annual rate of 2.8 percent. The cocoa sector has been the main driver of land expansion. The cocoa area has increased 1.7 times over the past 12 years, accounting for 60 percent of the total increase in area, while the remaining 40 percent of the total increase in cultivated land has been for all other crops.

Measured by the crop GDP in constant terms, land productivity did not increase in the past 12 years. Compared with the initial level in 1994, total

Box 4.1   Linkage effects through homegrown industrialization

Informal manufacturing activities often have strong domestic linkage effects and the potential to scale up and become important growth components in African countries. This scaling-up can be driven by domestic or international capital and entrepreneurs and requires significant improvements in the business environment. For example, the handloom sector in the cotton-production area of southern Ethiopia and the automobile-parts sector in the Magazine area of Ghana can be called informal, and thus have not been included in the countries' manufacturing-sector statistics.

There are many similarities between these examples and the textile and clothing industries in rural China, as well as the Christmas gift–producing sector in rural Thailand, during the early stages of transformation in these countries. One important commonality is that these manufacturing activities have been customized to the countries' initial comparative advantages. In addition, these activities have been established despite a series of initial disadvantages, such as a lack of financial capital and the existence of many other market and institutional barriers. Although similar constraints are faced by both the formal and the informal sectors, the informal sector often performs better than its formal counterpart in overcoming such initial constraints, and many informal enterprises have been established in extremely difficult economic and policy environments.

Given this dynamic history, these enterprises are likely to reach their full potential if governments take supportive policy and investment action to improve the private sector's business environment (that is, for both formal and informal groups). For example, improving infrastructural conditions, such as electricity and road access in the case of Ethiopia and removing credit constraints in the case of Ghana, should allow the previously mentioned informal manufacturing enterprises to grow rapidly, given the existence of a strong and growing demand from domestic markets. In this process, enterprises might also seek to establish links to the international market and to attract foreign capital, technology, and knowledge. Many textile and clothing products imported by the EU, the United States, and other developed countries today originate from Chinese, Thai, and Vietnamese villages, and some are even produced in farmers' houses.

Table 4.4 Subsectors' contribution to agricultural gross domestic product (AgGDP) growth in Ghana (percent), 1991-2006

Measure of growth, subsector	1991-95	1996-2000	2001-05	2006
Total annual growth	2.0	3.9	5.5	5.6
Crops other than cocoa	1.5	3.4	4.5	5.8
Cocoa production and marketing	7.0	6.0	14.8	8.3
Forestry and logging	1.9	10.8	5.1	2.5
Fishing	1.8	0.6	3.0	3.6
Share of AgGDP				
Crops other than cocoa	69	68	68	66
Cocoa production and marketing	8	9	10	13
Forestry and logging	7	9	10	10
Fishing	15	14	12	11
Contribution to agricultural GDP growth				
Crops other than cocoa	51	60	55	69
Cocoa production and marketing	28	14	28	19
Forestry and logging	7	24	9	4
Fishing	14	2	7	7

Source: Calculated using GSS (2007).
Note: GDP means gross domestic product.

Table 4.5 Land expansion and land productivity in Ghana, 1994-2006

Measure, type of land	1994	2000	2006	Overall growth rate, 1994-2006 (%)	Annual growth rate, 1994-99 (%)	Annual growth rate, 2000-06 (%)
Land productivity (cedi per hectare)[a]						
Crops and cocoa	155	112	159	0.91	-4.77	5.97
Cocoa	162	87	188	1.56	-10.49	13.67
Crops other than cocoa	154	121	149	0.69	-4.97	3.62
Land allocation (thousands of hectares)						
Cultivated land	4,500	6,100	7,195	4.10	5.39	2.79
Cocoa	687	1,500	1,835	7.01	13.62	3.42
Crops other than cocoa	3,813	4,600	5,360	3.31	3.59	2.58

Sources: Calculated using data from GSS (2007), FAO (2008), and IMF (2008).
[a]Land productivity is calculated as gross domestic product at constant 2000 prices divided by hectares of cultivated land. The value is reported in new Ghana cedi.

Table 4.6   Yields of major crops in Ghana by agroecological zone (metric tons per hectare), 1994-2005

Zone	Maize		Rice		Cassava	
	1994-97	2002-05	1994-97	2002-05	1994-97	2002-05
Coastal	1.32	1.69	3.64	2.16	10.46	13.02
Forest	1.45	1.48	1.79	1.99	7.37	8.25
Northern Savannah	1.21	1.16	1.94	2.22	7.07	9.26
Southern Savannah	1.53	1.44	2.09	2.24	9.01	7.54
Nation	1.51	1.56	1.94	2.18	11.87	12.53

Sources: Ghana, MoFA (2007) for zonal-level data and FAO (2008) for national data.

land productivity actually fell between 1997 and 2002 and recovered only in recent years, primarily driven by the growth in cocoa (see Table 4.5).

Although structural change in crop production helps to improve land productivity, the dominant factor by which to measure land productivity is yield growth. In contrast to rapid land expansion, national yield levels of major foodcrops in Ghana have improved only modestly over the past 12 years (Table 4.6). When looking at the yield levels of the agroecological zones, in several cases yields even fell in recent years from their levels in the mid-1990s. For example, maize yield increased only in the Coast Zone and was stagnant and even fell in the other three zones of the country.

These yields are much lower than the achievable yields for many crops in most zones of Ghana and provide an opportunity for agricultural growth. According to the MoFA, yields for most crops are 20-60 percent below their achievable levels under existing technologies combined with the use of modern inputs such as fertilizers and improved seeds (Table 4.7).

On the demand side, opportunities also exist to support agricultural growth in Ghana. Like those of many other African countries, Ghanaian households spend 40-50 percent of their incomes on food.[3] Food demand from the domestic market is expected to grow further with income and population growth and the process of urbanization (Diao et al. 2007). There are also considerable potentials for import substitution through increased competitiveness. Ghana imports 60 percent of the rice and 90 percent of the poultry meat consumed domestically. Demand for these two commodities is highly income elastic, indi-

---

[3] We use the recent national household survey, GLSS5 (2005-06) (GSS 2007) for the analysis. See Appendix A for expenditure patterns.

Table 4.7   Yield gaps in Ghana, 1990-2006

Crop	Average yields (metric tons/ hectare)	Achievable yields (metric tons/ hectare)	Yield gap (metric tons/ hectare)	Yield gap (%)
Maize	1.5	2.5	1.0	40.0
Rice	2.1	3.5	1.4	40.0
Millet	0.8	1.5	0.7	46.7
Sorghum	1.0	1.5	0.5	33.3
Cassava	11.9	28.0	16.1	57.5
Cocoyams	6.7	8.0	1.3	16.3
Yams	12.4	20.0	7.6	38.0
Plantains	8.1	10.0	1.9	19.0
Sweetpotatoes	8.5	18.0	9.5	52.8
Cowpeas	1.0	1.3	0.3	23.1
Groundnuts	0.8	1.0	0.2	20.0
Soybeans	0.8	1.0	0.2	20.0
Cocoa	0.4	1.0	0.6	60.0

Source: Ghana, MoFA (2007).
Note: According to MoFA's definition, achievable yields are derived from on-farm observations, where recommended technologies have been used together with more effective extension services.

cating that there will be an increase in imports in the future without improvements in domestic competitiveness. Moreover, as Brazil, Malaysia, Thailand, and many other developing countries have demonstrated, rapid diversification of agricultural exports is possible and can help to accelerate growth in agriculture and economic transformation in general (Breisinger and Diao 2008).

The foregoing analysis suggests that there is great potential for both agricultural and manufacturing growth in Ghana, whereas alternative growth options may have different outcomes. Thus, in the following chapters we develop an economywide model to quantitatively assess these potentials and measure the possible outcomes of realizing these potentials in helping Ghana achieve its development goal of transforming to a MIC in the next 10 years.

CHAPTER **5**

Modeling Productivity-Led Growth
and Its Implications for Transformation:
Methodology and Data

The Economywide Model in the Literature

A   lthough descriptive comparative studies on the theory and practice
    of transformation have become more prominent in recent years,
    quantitatively assessing alternative development paths has started to
make important contributions to the better understanding of the constraints,
trade-offs, and linkage effects of country-specific growth options. In this
regard, general equilibrium theory is a particularly relevant tool for understanding structural change due to its ability to incorporate intersectoral and
economywide linkages.

Accordingly, there have been several efforts among economists in recent
years to empirically study structural change using general equilibrium models.
For example, Irz and Roe (2005) build a two-sector growth model and calibrate
it to an archetype low-income economy. They find that low agricultural productivity can be an important bottleneck to overall growth, which primarily works
through high food prices and low savings rates. Echevarria (1997) develops a
Solow-type dynamic general equilibrium model to study changes in sectoral
composition and finds that structural change is driven by consumer preferences. Diao, Rattsø, and Stokke (2005) explicitly include international trade in
their intertemporal general equilibrium model to demonstrate the importance
of openness for structural change and growth. Most studies, however, analyze
structural change in an aggregate economy. Irz and Roe's (2005) model aggre-
gates its archetypal economy into two sectors, agriculture and nonagriculture.
Echevarria's (1997) model considers three sectors—the primary (agriculture
and mining), manufacturing, and service sectors—for several countries in the
Organisation for Economic Co-operation and Development. The model of Diao,
Rattsø, and Stokke (2005) for Thailand includes four sectors: agriculture,
exportables, importables, and nontradable nonagriculture. Although highly
aggregated general equilibrium models are helpful for understanding the gen-

eral driving forces of structural change, they ignore many country-specific factors critical to determining alternative growth paths that countries may follow
in their development processes. For example, initial economic structures are
quite different across countries, and such initial conditions often affect the set
of choices facing different countries.

To address this gap in the literature and to help Ghana in diagnosing its
strategic options for reaching MIC status, we developed a dynamic general
equilibrium model based on the most recent data available. The model
includes many economic sectors, some of which are currently important for
the national economy or for subnational regions and some that are expected
to become more important during the transformation process.

A Dynamic Computable General Equilibrium Model

The ability to capture inter-sector synergies, trade-offs and linkages has
made general equilibrium models an important tool to analyze the impacts of
growth accelerations. We therefore developed a recursive dynamic computable general equilibrium (DCGE) model to assess the sector-specific growth
options and their structural impact on the Ghanaian economy over a period
of 10–15 years. Although this model does not attempt to make precise predic-
tions about the future development of the Ghanaian economy, it does measure the roles of industrial, service, and agricultural growth in economywide
growth and structural change.

The DCGE model is constructed consistent with the neoclassical general
equilibrium theory. The theoretical background and the analytical framework
of computable general equilibrium (CGE) models have been well documented
in Dervis, de Melo, and Robinson (1982), while the detailed mathematical
presentation of a static CGE model is described in Lofgren, Harris, and Robinson (2002). The recursive dynamic version of the CGE model is based on this
standard CGE model with the incorporation of a series of dynamic factors.
The early version of this dynamic CGE model can be found in Thurlow (2004),
while its recent applications are included in Diao et al. (2007).

Similar to other CGE models, our DCGE model is an economywide, multi-
sectoral model that simultaneously and endogenously solves for a series of
economic variables including commodity and factor prices. However, unlike
traditional CGE models that focus on national economies with multiple production sectors, our DCGE model considers subnational heterogeneity in agricultural production by assigning a series of different production functions for
producing a similar agricultural product, for example, maize or cassava, to
different zones (regions). In the case of Ghana, four agroeclological zones—
Coastal, Forest, Southern Savannah, and Northern Savannah—are considered.
The setup of such a model requires more information about a country's agri-

cultural production than does a traditional CGE model, for instance, information about the distribution of land across zones for each individual type of crop or livestock production, which significantly increases the complexity of calibrating the model to the real economy. However, once such information is available and the model is constructed, the model can better capture the economic interlinkages at both subnational and national levels, including both linkages across regions and those between sectors. The specific subnational structure of the agricultural production of the model will be further discussed in detail later in this chapter when we introduce the dataset, the Ghana social accounting matrix, and the agricultural structure.

Like any other CGE model, the DCGE model captures, with its general equilibrium feature, economic activities on both the supply and the demand sides. On the supply side, the model has defined specific production functions for each economic activity, such as agricultural production, for which functions are defined at the subnational level, or nonagricultural production, which is defined only at the national level. As in any other quantitative economic analysis, certain assumptions have to be applied before calibrating the model to the data. In a typical general equilibrium model, a constant return to scale technology with constant elasticity of substitution between primary inputs is a fundamentally necessary assumption in order for the model to have an equilibrium solution.[1] However, because both primary and intermediate inputs are considered in the production functions of a CGE model, a Leontief technology with fixed input-output coefficients is often assumed for intermediate inputs, such as fertilizer and seeds in crop production, feed in animal production, and raw materials in the food processing industry, as well as for the relationship between intermediates and primary inputs in aggregation.

---

[1] The constant returns to scale assumption is a commonly used assumption in general equilibrium theory as well as in most applied general equilibrium models (including CGE models). This assumption follows a more fundamental assumption in neoclassical economics theory, that firms act in a perfectly competitive market and cannot fail to gain market power to determine input or output prices (all prices are the result of a market clearing mechanism [equilibrium] rather than of the choice of any individual firms). In some general equilibrium models, especially the models based on the new (or endogenous) growth theory, there is externality through the accumulation of common knowledge gained as a result of research and development activities conducted by individual firms (Romer 1990; Grossman and Helpman 1992) or through the accumulation of human capital (see Arrow 1962, for the famous learning-by-doing model). The existence of such externalities is the driving force of productivity growth in endogenous growth theory, but it is irrelevant to the market power of any firm. The increasing returns to scale assumption from microeconomics theory (which also relates to the creation of externalities from one firm to others) is not suitable to the general equilibrium theory unless this assumption is accompanied by the imperfect competition assumption, such that the choice variable for these firms is the price or market power instead of output (and inputs). Hence we follow this commonly used and theoretically consistent assumption in our CGE model.

The demand functions in the CGE model are derived from well-defined utility functions. In our model, the consumer demand functions are solved by means of a Stone–Geary type of utility function in which the income elasticity departs from one (which is a typical assumption in a Cobb–Douglas [C-D] type of utility function), and hence the marginal budget share (MBS) of each good consumed differs from its respective average budget share (ABS).[2] Moreover, we include highly disaggregated representative households in the model. Specifically, there are 90 representative households, 40 in the rural areas and 50 in the urban areas. The 40 rural households represent rural households in the four disaggregated zones and 10 income decile groups within each zone. For the urban households, beside the 40 zonal representative households, we also consider 10 income decile groups for the Greater Accra area, because households' income level and consumption patterns in Great Accra are quite different from those of other urban households in the other urban centers.

Much as in other general equilibrium models, consumers' income that enters the demand system is an endogenous variable. Income generated from the primary factors employed in the production process is the dominant income source for consumers, although the model also considers incomes from abroad (as remittances received) or the government (as direct transfers). Information on income distribution from labor and land derived from GLSS5 (GSS 2007) is used to calibrate the initial income distribution of the model. In general, most returns to land, labor, and capital employed in agricultural production at the regional level go to the region's rural household groups, while returns to capital employed in nonagricultural production and wage income for skilled labor go to urban households. Rural households also earn labor income from nonagricultural activities, which can be performed in either rural (that is, rural nonfarm) or urban areas.

With highly disaggregated demand systems derived from nonhomothetic functions, together with endogenous income growth, the DCGE model is able

---

[2] MBS relates the allocation of incremental income spent on different consumption goods by a consumer, while ABS is the current (total) budget allocation among different goods. For example, a consumer currently spends 2 percent of her income on rice consumption, indicating that the ABS of rice is 2 percent. When this consumer's income increases in the next year, for each dollar of increased income she chooses to spend 3 cents on rice. In this case, the MBS of rice is 3 percent. When MBS is greater than ABS for a particular consumption good (in this case, rice), demand for this good is called income elastic (Wilhelmsson 2002). On the other hand, if the MBS is lower than the ABS for a particular good, like sorghum, demand for this good (sorghum) is said to be income inelastic. The MBS is obtained by estimating income elasticities, using the household survey data (GLSS5) (GSS 2007), as the ratio of ABS or MBS equal to the income elasticity of this particular commodity. The estimation of income elasticities will be discussed later in this chapter.

to partially capture the Engel's Law effect of structural change led by consumers' preferences, while supply-side factors that lead to structural change are primarily productivity growth that will be discussed later.

The DCGE model explicitly models the relationship between supply and demand, which determines the equilibrium prices in domestic markets. Given that a CGE model reflects an open economy and hence also captures the trade flows—both imports and exports—the relationship between domestic and international markets is included explicitly. Generally speaking, any commodity produced or consumed in the domestic market can also be exported or imported. However, in a CGE model the commodities produced or consumed domestically are not perfectly substitutable for internationally traded goods. Thus the international price for any product, regardless of whether this product is exportable or importable, is not fully transmitted into domestic markets; rather, changes in domestic supply and demand will finally determine its price. However, if a product is exportable or importable, its price in domestic markets can be affected by international prices and by export and import demands. To capture the linkages between the domestic and international markets, the model assumes price-sensitive substitution (imperfect substitution) between foreign goods and domestic production. With such an assumption, if domestic demand increases more than the supply of a good, the domestic price for this good rises relative to the export/import prices. Exports of this good decrease, and imports increase. On the other hand, if productivity improves for domestic production and rising supply outpaces the increases in demand for the product, the domestic price falls relative to the border prices, exports increase, and imports decrease. Imperfect substitution also implies that agricultural productivity improvements by themselves may not be enough to expand agricultural exports and that improving marketing conditions is also important.

Although the linkages between demand and supply through changes in income (an endogenous variable) and productivity (often an exogenous variable) are the most important general equilibrium interactions in an economywide model, production linkages also occur across sectors through intermediate demand and competition for primary factors employed in the production sectors. Many primary agricultural products need to be processed before reaching consumers and export markets. Food processing is often an important component of the manufacturing sector in developing countries. Productivity-led growth in the agricultural sector can stimulate growth in food processing by providing cheap inputs (forward linkages) and creating more demand for processed goods (backward linkages through the rising incomes of farmers). On the other hand, growth in an export-oriented agricultural product, for example, cocoa in Ghana, often creates increased demand for cocoa processing. Although most of such processing activities create very little value addition, they increase labor demand and hence create job opportunities for both rural and urban households. Clearly, without a general equilibrium framework and detailed subsector structure in both agriculture and nonagriculture, this economywide impact of agricultural growth might not be captured.

The focus of this monograph is economic transformation. Thus, it is important to clarify which parts of the transformation process can be captured by DCGE models and where the model's weaknesses are. As we discussed in Chapter 3, transformation is commonly accompanied by rapid economic growth, and such growth is productivity driven with increased capital investment. As in most recursive dynamic models, productivity growth is an exogenous variable in our DCGE model, while investment in capital formation is an endogenous process led by profitability. The accumulation of investment is financed by domestic private and public savings, as well as by foreign inflows. Given the complexity of the model setup for Ghana in terms of its large number of production sectors in both agriculture and nonagriculture and its highly disaggregated agricultural production and household groups across subnational regions, it is unrealistic to develop a fully intertemporal general equilibrium model for this study.[3] In a recursive dynamic model (like the one developed for this monograph), the dynamics occur between only two periods at a time. There are two types of capital, agricultural and nonagricultural, and the intraperiod of agricultural and nonagricultural capital allocation across different agricultural and nonagricultural subsectors is driven by within-period sectoral profitability. The allocation of investment to these two types of capital is based on the previous period's total returns of each type of capital. Total investment is determined by the available savings, including domestic savings and foreign inflows. A Solow type of saving decision is assumed, such that the private savings of each representative household are proportional to that household's income. Although the savings rate is constant, with income increases over time, the amount of private savings grow. The government savings are a residual term that is given by the difference between total government expenditure, which is an exogenous variable, and total government income, an endogenous variable. Foreign inflows to finance domestic investment (through either FDI or other financial inflows) are considered an exogenous variable in the model. Changes in foreign inflows in the model's base run are consistent with inflows observed in recent years.

---

[3] An intertemporal general equilibrium model in the literature is often used with a relatively aggregated economic structure. See Diao, Rattsø, and H. E. Stokke (2005) for the growth linkage analysis in the case of Thailand as an example.

In the scenarios for future structural change that we present in Chapter 6, we have considered possible increases in foreign inflows when accelerated growth is led by expansion and growth in the industrial or the service sector. These increases are compatible with Ghana's expected better access to official development assistance and private foreign funds in the future. The main reasons for the expected improvement in foreign inflows are the government's strong commitment to macroeconomic stability and the discovery of oil, which is expected to boost government revenues. The effects of the discovery of oil will be further discussed once we introduce the model simulations later in the next chapter.

As discussed in Chapter 3, although productivity and capital accumulation have led transformation characterized by changes in economic structure, the process of transformation goes beyond the structural change among productive sectors. Demographic transformation occurs simultaneously during transformation. Thus it is necessary to understand how the model can capture both economic structural change and demographic transformation. As we briefly mentioned earlier, two forces drive the economic structural change in the model: changes in the domestic demand structure led by Engel's Law (by introducing a nonhomothetic utility function in the model) and differential growth rates (led by productivity change) across sectors. Moreover, in the general equilibrium model, these two forces work together through interactions between demand and supply in domestic markets. Differential growth rates at the sector level are not purely determined by the productivity increase within each sector but are also constrained by the demand side, especially if the sector does not export. For example, although we can exogenously set a high productivity growth rate for a particular sector (for example, cassava), under Engel's Law, demand for cassava may not grow proportionally to growing incomes. Thus, in the absence of export opportunities or new ways to process and use cassava in the manufacturing sector, the price of cassava falls due to oversupply in the domestic market. As a consequence of falling prices, production factors (labor, land, and capital) leave cassava production until growth in supply matches consumer demand.

As discussed in Chapter 3, demographic transformation is characterized by the population shift from rural to urban areas. Although it is important to capture such a shift, this process is unlikely to be fully determined endogenously in the model. Thus we have to combine an exogenous assumption about growth in labor supply with the endogenous general equilibrium process of agriculture-nonagriculture labor mobility. Specifically, we exogenously determined the annual growth rate for different types of labor supply based on Ghana's historical trends in labor growth. Three types of labor are considered based on the employment information of GLSS5 (GSS 2007). Family labor is employed in agricultural production only and is specific to one of the agroecological zones. Unskilled and skilled labor are economywide factors, that is, these two factors can move freely between regions and sectors following the highest returns. According to the Food and Agriculture Organization of the United Nations (FAO), the agricultural labor force currently accounts for 60 percent of the total economically active population in Ghana, while the agricultural labor share has declined over time. We conducted a simple regression between the change in agricultural labor share and agricultural TFP. The regression results show that growth of 1 percent in agricultural TFP is associated with 0.07 percent decline in the share of agricultural labor in the total labor force. Using this elasticity, together with projected total labor growth between 2007 and 2020 (drawn from FAO), we calibrate the growth rate in total agricultural labor supply, which declines over time. That is, agricultural family labor supply grows at 1.7 percent annually in the early years in the model and slows to 1.1 percent by 2020. On the other hand, unskilled and skilled labor supplies, both of which are mobile economywide factors (that is, between agriculture and nonagriculture), grow at 3.4 and 3.6 percent, respectively, in the early model years, and the growth rate rises to 3.7 percent for the unskilled labor supply and 4.2 percent for the skilled labor supply by 2020. In total, labor supply will grow at 2.7 percent initially and slow down to 2.5 percent by 2020, which is consistent with FAO's projections.

Although the supply of labor increases in each time period according to the exogenously set growth rate discussed earlier, labor demand at the subsector level is determined by the sector's profitability at given wage rates. Individual producers in both the agricultural and the nonagricultural production sectors treat wages as given. The wage rate is an endogenous variable determined by the market equilibrium between total labor supply and total labor demand. Accordingly, there are four different wage rates for family labor (one for each agroecological zone) and one wage rate for skilled and unskilled labor, respectively. Wage rates change over time, driven by changes in labor demand across sectors. For example, if overall economic growth is led by labor-intensive sectors (for example, textiles), additional demand for labor from these sectors can cause wage rates to rise relative to the returns to the other factors (for example, capital). On the other hand, if growth is led by sectors that are highly capital intensive (for example, oil extraction), demand for labor may not increase much during the growth process ("jobless growth"). Given similar labor supply growth, wage rates may thus fall or rise less than the returns to capital, depending on the driving sector of growth. Whether or not the wage rate (particularly the wage rate for family and unskilled labor) rises during periods of growth affects income distribution and poverty reduction during transformation. This will be further discussed in the description of the simulations and results.

Although the exogenously determined differences in growth rates for various types of labor partially capture the demographic patterns of transformation, the movement of economywide labor (skilled and unskilled labor) between agricultural and nonagricultural sectors is an important factor in endogenously capturing rural–urban (or agriculture–nonagriculture) labor mobility. In general, we expect more demand for nonagricultural labor than for agricultural labor in the transformation process due to the demand- and supply-side factors discussed earlier. On the demand side, given that most agricultural consumption goods are generally income inelastic and most nonagricultural goods are income elastic, demand for nonagricultural products (including services) grows more rapidly. On the supply side, productivity growth in the agricultural sector generally releases labor from agriculture to nonagriculture, because agricultural growth is also constrained by the natural resource conditions (particular land). Productivity growth in the nonagricultural sectors, particularly manufacturing and services, faces fewer natural resource constraints, and these sectors may thus hire new laborers (if they are not constrained by capital). In the next chapter of the monograph, we will further analyze this labor shift process in Ghana.

A Social Accounting Matrix (SAM) for Ghana

The DCGE model is calibrated to a 2007 SAM that is an updated version of the Ghana 2005 SAM. A detailed description of the data sources and the balancing procedure of the 2005 Ghana SAM can be downloaded from IFPRI's website (Breisinger, Thurlow, and Duncan 2007). A wide range of data was used to build the 2005 SAM, including national accounts provided by GSS; crop and livestock data provided by MoFA; mining-, manufacturing-, and energy-sector data from the 2003 Industrial Census (GSS); household income and consumption data from GLSS5; and export and import data provided by the Bank of Ghana, MoFA, and GSS. To update this SAM to 2007, we use national account data from 2007 provided by GSS, balance-of-payments data provided by the Bank of Ghana, and government budget data provided by the Ministry of Finance.

The newly developed Ghana SAM provides information on the demand and production structures of 70 detailed sectors, including 27 agricultural subsectors, 33 industrial subsectors, and 10 service subsectors (see Table D.1 for a list of the subsectors). This detailed sector structure allows the DCGE model to analyze sector- and subsector-specific growth strategies and their contribution to economic transformation. As we briefly mentioned earlier, and consistent with the DCGE model, the SAM considers the existence of different types of labor forces, such as agricultural family labor (or self-employed agricultural workers), unskilled workers employed in both agriculture and nonagriculture, and skilled nonagricultural workers. Information on sector-level inputs and outputs is further derived from MoFA's 2006 crop-level farm budgets for the agricultural sectors and from the 2003 Industrial Census for industrial production. Additional information on employment and wages by sector and region is taken from GLSS5 (Ghana, MoFA 2007). The SAM and the DCGE model include a government account, which collects direct taxes from households and indirect taxes from imports, exports, and domestic sales and then supplements its revenues with foreign grants from development partners that are used for investment expenditures. Information on government revenues and expenditures was provided by the Ministry of Finance and Economic Planning.

Elasticities and Parameters

In addition to the SAM as the main data source to calibrate to a set of parameters in both production and demand functions, a DCGE model also requires several elasticities. The main elasticities include the substitution elasticity between primary inputs in the value-added production function, the elasticity between domestically produced and consumed goods and exported or imported goods, and the income elasticity in the demand functions. Although we briefly discuss the main assumptions and the sources for these elasticities, a sensitivity test is conducted in order to assess the robustness of these elasticities (which is further discussed in Appendix F).

The assumption of a constant elasticity of substitution (CES) technology in the production function requires a substitution elasticity that is generally not possible to estimate using country-specific econometrics given the highly disaggregate production structure of a DCGE model. This substitution elasticity is not needed if a C-D technology is chosen for the production functions. However, C-D functions implicitly imply that the substitution elasticity between two inputs (for example, labor and land) is one, which is not a suitable assumption in a general equilibrium model with a highly disaggregated production structure. Thus the CES elasticity in the production function has to be predetermined and drawn from the CGE literature on other African countries. The other parameters or coefficients in the production functions of the model (for example, the marginal product of each input) can be directly calibrated using the country data of the Ghana SAM (for example, the share of value added for each input used in the total value added of this sector).

For the use of intermediate inputs in the production function, we use a Leontief technology. With this assumption, a set of fixed input-output co-efficients can be directly derived using the data of the Ghana SAM.

As we briefly discussed earlier, with a Stone–Geary type of nonhomothetic utility function applied in the model, MBS is the parameter applied in the demand system, which can be derived from the SAM given that the income elasticity of demand is known. The income elasticity is estimated from a semi-log inverse function suggested by King and Byerlee (1978) and based on the data of GLSS 5 (2005–06) (GSS 2007).[4] Using the estimated results, together with the average budget share for each individual commodity consumed by each individual household group, directly calculated using the data of the Ghana SAM, we derive a series of MBSs that are applied in the model (see Appendix E for a series of elasticities, including the income elasticities that are used to derive MBSs in the model).

For commodities that are sold both domestically and abroad, a constant elasticity of transformation function is applied, while for commodities that have both domestic and foreign supply, a CES or Armington function is used. In both functional forms, the elasticity of substitution that represents the ease with which producers or consumers are willing to shift supply or demand between domestic and foreign markets is required. With minor modifications, these elasticities have been adopted from Hertel et al. (2007), who estimated average import substitution elasticities for 40 commodities from a large set of countries.

Limitations of the DCGE Model

Like any other economic model, the CGE model has its limitations. Of these, there are at least four limitations or caveats that are important to note when interpreting the results. The first caveat has to do with the way to construct the dataset (the SAM) for CGE modeling analysis. Unlike in a typical econometric analysis, in which either time-series or cross-section data are used to estimate the causality relationship between economic and social variables, the dataset (the SAM) used in any CGE model analysis is constructed from one year's data. Given that the agricultural sector is one of the most important economic sectors in many African countries and agricultural production is predominantly influenced by patterns of rainfall and other weather-related factors that often fluctuate over time, the choice of the year used to construct the SAM matters. To avoid possible bias in the choice of the base year, it is necessary for CGE modeling researchers to assess the data for a longer time period for the main economic activities, particularly for agricultural production, to ensure that the year chosen for the study is a "normal" year.

---

[4] We greatly thank Bingxin Yu, who provided an econometric estimation of the income elasticity of demand in the study.

Although the original SAM for Ghana was constructed for the year 2005, we have carefully checked whether the year of 2005 is a representative year for Ghana's agriculture and have used the average production data over several years for most crop and livestock subsectors. We have also considered trends in total GDP, agricultural GDP, and agricultural production for major crops to ensure a proper reflection of the structure of the Ghanaian economy in the SAM at the sector level.

The second caveat applies to the model's treatment of consumers' demand. Although income elasticities of demand in the model are econometrically estimated and subsistence consumption is taken into account in the demand functions, the use of a linear expenditure system to specify household demand can only partially capture demand dynamics. Marginal budget shares in such a demand system remain constant over time. Although rapid demand shifts can be better captured using an implicitly directly additive demand system (Yu et al. 2003) or by applying latent separability (Gohin 2005), the highly disaggregated demand structure in the model constrains our choice of methods. The use of this relatively linear demand system can be questioned, particularly in the context of economic transformation, on the grounds that it might be too rigid to reflect rapid change. However, although the functional form, parameters, and elasticities applied to the demand functions are given, the level of consumption and relative demand, and hence the consumption shares of individual commodities, do change over time and thus reflect changes in incomes and relative prices (both income and prices are endogenous variables in the model). The major concern is thus whether these changes are great enough at times when the economy experiences periods of rapid structural change.

Third, as in most other CGE models, production technologies that are calibrated to the initial economic conditions remain constant over time. That is to say, as in the demand system, the production functional forms, including the parameters and elasticities of the functions, are given. That does not imply a constant economic structure over time, because the share of each production sector in the overall economy changes with productivity growth and price evolution, varying across sectors and over time. However, with the given production functions, the model simulations cannot capture the substantial technological changes and innovations that may be embodied in new investments, especially FDI, which technically involve changes in the functional forms for some more dynamic production sectors. Given that foreign investments currently account for only an insignificant portion of Ghana's GDP, this caveat may be less relevant to the study.

The fourth caveat is that although the model captures the market equilibrium and linkages between domestic and foreign markets, it does not consider the role of market institutions and other players (beside producers and consumers) along the supply chains or spatial characteristics of the markets. Although including detailed service subsectors (for example, trade, transport) helps the model partially capture the linkages between service activities and other production sectors and between consumption and export/import activities, these linkages are mainly treated as a sort of production linkage (that is, services are inputs in other types of production) or as directly consumed by households. Because of this caveat, the model may underestimate the important role of the service sectors in supporting growth in the other sectors and hence the sector's contribution to broad economic growth. As discussed in Chapter 3, transformation is also a process of institutional change. However, given the model's neoclassical nature, it cannot properly reflect institutional change both as one of the most important conditions for and as an outcome of transformation.

We have to point out that the four caveats discussed here are common to most CGE models, and some of them are rooted in the general equilibrium theory from which a numerical model is constructed. However, it is still worth explicitly pointing them out in order to help readers fully understand the model results and interpret them accordingly. With these limitations in mind, the next chapter discusses the model's results.

CHAPTER 6

Scenarios for Future Structural Change

In previous chapters we examined the structural transformation of selected developing countries that have successfully moved from situations similar to Ghana's today to MIC status. We have seen that although doubling the level of per capita incomes in 10–15 years is ambitious, it is not unprecedented. All the countries whose economic transformations are summarized in Chapter 2 experienced periods of rapid growth driven by productivity and capital accumulation. This growth has led to significant structural changes and rapid increases in the contribution of manufacturing to their overall economies, while only India experienced more rapid service-led growth. However, the literature and country experiences also suggest that agriculture has often played an important role in development, notably in the Green Revolution in Asia. Taken together, the experiences of successful countries suggest that there is no single path from low- to middle-income status and that the contribution of various sectors during each country's transformation process depended on the country's unique initial economic structures, existing and new market opportunities, other initial conditions embodied in social and political institutions and government policies, and external conditions in the region and the world, among other factors. Ghana has made great progress in all these areas over recent years, which might herald a new era of rapid growth and transformation.

We have designed five scenarios and used the DCGE model introduced in Chapter 5 to quantitatively assess Ghana's medium-term goal of reaching MIC status in the context of economic transformation. Scenario 1 is a base run in which we examine whether Ghana's current strong performance will be sufficient to achieve MIC status by 2020. In Scenario 2 we simulate the effects of rapid growth in industry (excluding mining), especially in "homegrown" and agriculture-related manufacturing sectors. In Scenario 3 we assess the impacts of growth led by private service (both domestic and export oriented). In Scenario 4 we argue that accelerated growth in agriculture is important given Ghana's economic structure and lessons from other countries. Specifically, in Scenario 4a we examine growth acceleration in export agriculture, while in Scenario 4b we turn to the growth in staple agriculture, which includes staple crops and livestock. Then in Scenario 4c we combine the two scenarios to assess overall agricultural growth. Finally, in Scenario 5 we combine all the previous scenarios and focus on the possible structural change facing Ghana as it strives to become a MIC. In all scenarios we exogenously assume additional growth in affected sectors' TFP. In the base run, the choice of growth rate for the sector-level TFP is based on the calibration, such that the economy will continue to grow along its historical path. After the base run, any additional growth is an assumption, that is, we do not try to model the growth in TFP. Instead, by exogenously changing the growth parameters in the TFP equation sector by sector, we analyze TFP growth-led economic structural change further through resource shifts (for example, labor and land reallocation), capital accumulation, and changes in demand structure. Table 6.1 provides an overview of the assumptions regarding TFP growth rate across sectors for different scenarios, which are further explained in the discussion of the results that follows.

Obviously, productivity change should be a result of either innovation/ adoption of technology applied in the production process or improvement of efficiency in the use of production inputs with a given technology. In addition to human and physical capital as important sources of productivity growth, institutional factors (including market development) are frequently seen

Table 6.1   Overview of growth scenario assumptions for Ghana

Scenario	Affected sector	Additional annual growth in sector's total factor productivity (as exogenous changes)
Scenario 2: Industry-led growth	Manufacturing	1.0-4.0
	Other industry (excluding mining)	1.0-3.0
Scenario 3: Service-led growth	Private services	1.0-3.0
Scenario 4: Agriculture-led growth		
4a Export-led growth	Export crops	1.5-4.0
4b Staples-led growth	Cereals	0.2-4.0
	Root crops	1.0-1.5
	Other staple crops	1.0-2.0
	Livestock	1.5-2.0
4c All agriculture	Combined scenarios 4a and 4b	Combined scenarios 4a and 4b
Scenario 5: Middle-income-country broad-based growth	Combined scenarios 1-4	Combined scenarios 1-4

Source: Authors, based on the Ghana computable general equilibrium model.

to relate to improvement in productivity. Although these are all important aspects in understanding "how" productivity can grow, they are beyond the scope of this monograph. Moreover, the financing mechanism for productivity growth is also an important aspect in the development literature. In a general equilibrium theory, such a financing mechanism also affects the macro-economic balance and hence possibly results in certain unexpected outcomes in terms of growth. In this monograph we ignore this issue and do not model the investment and financing required for productivity growth.

Scenario 1: Business-as-Usual

The DCGE model is first applied to Scenario 1 (the base run), in which the sector-level growth rate is close to the growth trends observed in recent years (between 2001 and 2008). For agriculture, we consider a relatively higher growth rate compared to historical trends, and in the service sector we consider a lower growth rate to achieve a rather balanced growth path in the base run. If it follows the base-run growth path, Ghana's economy will continue to grow at an annual rate of 5.6 percent until 2020 (Table 6.2, Part A). Given the average annual rate of population growth of 2.2–2.3 percent, Ghana's per capita GDP, measured in U.S. dollars, will increase from \$587 in 2007 to \$838 by 2020 (Table 6.2, Part D) under this scenario.[1]

The results from this base-run scenario also show that the agricultural sector will continue to be an important contributor to overall growth, accounting for 29.3 percent of total growth (see Table 6.2, Part B). As expected under this growth scenario, the economic structure will not change. The shares of the three economic sectors in total GDP will remain relatively constant and thus reflect a balanced growth path (see Table 6.2, Part C).

We further investigate the sources of growth in this scenario. Growth is the outcome of increased labor supply, expansion of agricultural cropland, accumulation of capital, and improvement in TFP. As discussed in Chapter 5, increases in labor supply for various labor categories are set exogenously. The supply of agricultural family labor is assumed to grow more slowly than that of other unskilled and skilled labor to reflect rural–urban migration patterns. Land expansion is defined at the zonal level and varies between 1.2 percent and 3.1 percent across the four zones according to recent historical trends. This results in an average annual land expansion rate of 2.3 percent for the total cropland in the country. TFP growth is exogenously defined for each sector and varies across sectors. The increase in labor and land supply,

---

[1] The population growth rate in the model starts at 2.32 percent in 2008 and falls to 2.23 percent by 2020.

Table 6.2 Base-run and accelerated-growth scenarios for Ghana

Scenario, sector	Initial value	Base run	Scenarios with growth in:						Middle-income country
			Industry	Services	Export agriculture	Staples	All agriculture	
A. Annual growth rate, 2008-20 (%)									
Total GDP	5.7	5.6	6.5	6.4	5.8	5.9	6.1	7.7
Agriculture	3.2	4.6	4.3	4.5	5.5	5.6	6.3	6.1
Industry	5.0	5.7	8.8	5.6	5.6	5.7	5.5	8.5
Services	8.0	6.4	6.4	8.8	6.4	6.4	6.4	8.6
B. Sector's contribution to GDP growth (%)									
Agriculture		29.3	22.1	24.6	34.4	33.3	37.7	27.0
Industry		30.9	44.5	25.9	28.2	28.9	26.5	33.8
Services		39.8	33.4	49.5	37.4	37.8	35.8	39.1
C. Sector's share of GDP by 2020 (%)									
Agriculture	35.1	35.2	33.1	34.3	37.0	35.1	36.9	34.0
Industry	30.5	30.1	33.2	28.9	29.0	30.0	28.9	30.7
Services	34.4	34.7	33.6	36.8	34.0	34.9	34.2	35.4
D. Per capita income by 2020 (current US$)									
Total GDP	587	838	938	938	870	852	883	1,041
Agriculture	206	295	311	322	322	299	326	354
Industry	179	252	312	271	252	255	255	319
Services	202	291	316	345	296	297	303	369

Source: Authors, based on Ghana dynamic computable general equilibrium model results.
Note: GDP means gross domestic product.

combined with improvements in TFP, stimulate investment and result in an average annual capital accumulation growth rate of 5.9 percent.

Table 6.3 summarizes the contribution of each factor to GDP growth. Increases in labor explain 39.3 percent of the base-run growth over the next 13 years (2008–20), while land expansion explains 6.6 percent and capital 28.9 percent. About a quarter of growth is explained by productivity growth in the base run, which is consistent with World Bank estimates using data from the past five years (Bogetic et al. 2007).

According to the information reported in the national accounts, the ratio of investment to GDP was 28.5 percent in Ghana in 2007 (Table 6.4). The model calibrates to this ratio as an initial condition. In the base-run scenario, the ratio declines slightly to 25.5 percent by 2020. The data show that the

Table 6.3   Sources of gross domestic product growth in Ghana as in model results (percent of total), 2008-20

| Source of growth | Base run | Scenarios with growth in: | | | | All agriculture | Middle-income country |
		Industry	Services	Export agriculture	Staples		
Labor	39.3	34.9	32.3	36.9	38.8	36.5	30.3
Land	6.6	4.5	4.5	9.0	7.1	9.3	6.7
Capital	28.9	28.3	24.5	28.0	28.6	27.8	25.7
Productivity	25.1	32.4	38.7	26.1	25.5	26.4	37.3

Source: Authors, based on Ghana dynamic computable general equilibrium model results.

Table 6.4   Sources of investment in Ghana as in model results (percent of total), 2020

| Source of investment | Initial value in 2007 | Base run | Scenarios with growth in: | | | | All agriculture | Middle-income country |
			Industry	Services	Export agriculture	Staples		
Investment / gross domestic product	28.5	25.5	25.7	27.2	25.7	25.5	25.7	27.0
Share of investment	100.0	100.0	100.0	100.0	100.0	100.0	100.0	100.0
Foreign inflows	3.1	3.7	4.3	3.6	3.6	3.7	3.5	3.7
Private savings	53.4	59.6	57.8	54.6	59.0	59.4	58.9	53.8
Government spending	43.5	36.7	37.9	41.9	37.4	36.9	37.6	42.5

Source: Authors, based on Ghana dynamic computable general equilibrium model results.

government is a primary investor in Ghana and that the major sources of government investment are inflows of foreign aid and grants. According to national accounts, the government is responsible for 43.5 percent of investment spending, while private savings account for 53.4 percent of total investment. The remainder comes from non-government-related foreign inflows, including FDI, which accounts for a minor share (3.1 percent) of total investment. Along the base-run growth path, which is consistent with Ghana's past record, the structure of investment remains relatively constant, with the exception that the share of private savings and foreign inflows in total investment increases slightly.

The base-run results underline the need to accelerate growth in Ghana if the country aims to more than double its per capita income in a period of 10–15 years. To understand how each sector's growth contributes to that goal and how a country's economic structure changes with accelerated growth across sectors, we exogenously and sequentially increased growth in various sectors in the remaining four scenarios, shown in Table 6.1. We start from industry-led growth.

Scenario 2: Industry-Led Growth and Structural Change

As discussed in Chapter 2, accelerated growth in the industrial sector, particularly the manufacturing sector, is often an important driver of overall growth on the way from low- to middle-income status. For example, when Thailand's per capita GDP increased from about $400 in 1976 to $970 in 1987 (see Table A.1), its average annual manufacturing growth rate was twice as high as its agricultural growth rate. A similar situation occurred in Brazil, where the manufacturing growth rate was three times the agricultural growth rate. In addition, lessons from many countries suggest that labor-intensive and "homegrown" manufacturing, that is, sectors in which most developing countries have a comparative advantage in the early stage of transformation, are most likely to become drivers of growth. Based on these experiences and to evaluate how accelerated growth in the industrial sectors will contribute to overall growth and structural transformation in Ghana, we exogenously increased productivity in various industrial sectors (excluding mining) in the model and assumed higher growth in the labor-intensive manufacturing sectors. To finance growth acceleration in manufacturing, we assumed that foreign inflows will increase to finance the increased demand for capital goods.

The industrial sector as a whole accounts for 30.5 percent of the economy in 2007 (see Table 6.2, Part B). If mining is excluded (and construction and utilities included), the share falls to 21 percent. Manufacturing alone accounts for about 10 percent of total GDP (see Table 4.1). Both numbers are similar to the corresponding shares in Malaysia in 1965. Industry's share of GDP is also similar to that of Thailand in 1976, India in 1992, and Vietnam in 1997. However, the share of manufacturing in these three countries' economies in those years was much higher than in Ghana's in 2007. Ghana's manufacturing accounted for less than 30 percent of its industrial GDP and was dominated by activities heavily dependent on agricultural inputs, such as food and wood processing. As a whole, agriculture-related manufacturing accounted for 64 percent of manufacturing GDP in 2007.

In Scenario 2 we accelerate industrial growth, especially in the manufacturing sectors (that is, food and wood processing, textiles, clothing, and footwear). Most of the agriculture-related manufacturing sectors are labor intensive and are expected to generate more labor demand, which is an important factor explaining the structural change in employment among successfully transforming developing countries. Growth in the manufacturing sector is also expected to increase the sector's exports and decrease its imports such that more domestic demand will be satisfied by domestic production rather than by imports. This will further affect the trade structure of the country. In 2007, manufacturing as a whole exported only 15.9 percent of its production (Table 6.5, Part A), generating 14.2 percent of the country's total exports (Table 6.6, Part A). Agriculture-related manufacturing was more export intensive because exports were equivalent to 27.6 percent of the sector's output value (see Table 6.5, Part A). On the other hand, domestic demand for manufacturing was heavily dependent on imports, which accounted for 56.6 percent of domestic manufacturing consumption in 2007 (see Table 6.5, Part B) and for 92.4 percent of total imports (see Table 6.6, Part B). However, the share of imports in agriculture-related manufacturing consumption was relatively low, about 40.9 percent of domestic consumption (see Table 6.5). A precondition for accelerated manufacturing growth in Ghana is therefore improvement of the sector's global or regional competitiveness such that its exports increase or imports decline.

With exogenously increased productivity, the average annual growth rate for industrial GDP rises to 8.8 percent from 5.7 percent in the base run. In particular, in Scenario 2 growth in manufacturing production accelerates to 10.2 percent and in agriculture-related manufacturing to 11.6 percent (Table 6.7, Part B). Compared with the base-run scenario, the growth rate for manufacturing in this scenario is 4.1 percentage points higher and for agriculture-related manufacturing is 5.1 percentage points higher. Increased productivity in the country's manufacturing sector allows the sector to hire more labor relative to capital given its labor-intensive structure. Competition with other sectors in hiring labor also attracts new capital investments such that productivity-led growth results in capital accumulation and hence further enhances the sector's growth.

Table 6.5 Relationship between trade and domestic production/consumption in Ghana in model results (percent), 2020

Sector, subsector	Initial value in 2007	Base run	Scenarios with growth in:					Middle-income country
			Industry	Services	Export agriculture	Staples	All agriculture	
A. Exports								
Total exports / gross domestic product (GDP)	36.3	39.2	39.7	43.4	40.7	38.2	39.6	41.7
Total agricultural exports / value of agricultural production	26.4	25.8	20.8	25.8	31.2	24.7	30.0	24.2
Cocoa export quantity / cocoa production	87.3	84.1	82.5	86.6	85.7	83.6	85.3	84.2
Forestry export quantity / forestry production	73.2	78.8	62.3	80.4	82.8	78.8	82.4	65.6
Nonagricultural exports / value of nonagricultural production	15.9	17.5	19.8	19.5	16.4	17.3	16.1	19.3
Manufacturing exports / value of manufacturing production	14.9	15.3	21.1	12.3	13.6	15.9	14.0	20.2
Agriculture-related manufacturing exports / value of agriculture-related manufacturing production	27.6	27.8	35.4	23.6	25.4	28.4	25.7	34.0
B. Imports								
Total imports / GDP	61.9	61.4	59.8	63.3	62.0	60.0	60.6	59.8
Total agricultural imports / value of agricultural production	30.0	29.6	28.9	29.5	30.1	29.5	30.1	28.7
Rice import quantity / rice consumption	69.6	69.0	78.4	71.5	72.1	42.6	46.3	56.9
Poultry import quantity / poultry consumption	95.4	95.7	97.2	96.7	96.1	92.8	93.5	95.8
Nonagricultural imports / nonagricultural consumption	30.0	29.6	28.9	29.5	30.1	29.5	30.1	28.7
Manufacturing imports / manufacturing consumption	56.6	54.7	52.6	55.5	55.5	54.7	55.5	52.9
Agriculture-related manufacturing imports / agriculture-related manufacturing consumption	40.9	37.5	29.7	40.3	39.3	36.7	38.5	30.5

Source: Authors, based on Ghana dynamic computable general equilibrium model results.

Table 6.6 Structure of Ghana's exports and imports in model results (percent), 2020

Measure, sector	Initial value in 2007	Base run	Scenarios with growth in:					Middle-income country
			Industry	Services	Export agriculture	Staples	All agriculture	
A. Sector share in total exports								
Agriculture	39.7	36.5	27.7	32.8	44.6	35.7	43.8	43.8
Cocoa exports	25.7	20.2	16.8	18.2	25.2	20.1	25.2	25.2
Forestry exports	12.2	13.9	9.0	12.7	14.9	13.1	14.2	14.2
Nonagriculture	60.3	63.5	72.3	67.2	55.4	64.3	56.2	56.2
Mining	30.9	29.4	34.8	23.0	26.6	29.1	26.5	26.5
Manufacturing	14.2	14.9	23.6	10.2	12.0	16.1	12.8	12.8
Agriculture-related manufacturing	13.8	14.5	23.2	9.9	11.7	15.7	12.5	12.5
Service net exports	15.2	19.2	13.9	34.0	16.8	19.1	16.9	16.9
B. Sector share in total imports								
Agriculture	7.6	7.8	9.4	8.3	7.9	5.3	5.5	5.5
Rice	3.7	3.5	3.8	3.4	3.6	2.3	2.5	2.5
Poultry	1.0	1.2	1.2	1.3	1.2	1.2	1.2	1.2
Nonagriculture	92.4	92.2	90.6	91.7	92.1	94.7	94.5	94.5
Manufacturing	92.4	92.2	90.6	91.7	92.1	94.7	94.5	94.5
Agriculture-related manufacturing	18.6	17.8	13.9	18.5	18.3	18.0	18.4	18.4

Source: Authors, based on Ghana dynamic computable general equilibrium model results.

Table 6.7 Structure of Ghana's industry and its subsectors' contribution to industrial growth in model results (percent)

Measure, sector	Initial value in 2007	Base run	Scenarios with growth in: Industry	Services	Export agriculture	Staples	All agriculture	Middle-income country
A. Structure of industry, 2020								
Industrial share of GDP	30.5	30.1	33.2	28.9	29.0	30.0	28.9	30.7
Share in industrial GDP								
Construction	34.5	29.5	23.6	33.8	31.1	29.9	31.5	27.9
Manufacturing	33.2	37.3	42.5	34.8	35.9	37.5	36.1	43.8
Agriculture-related manufacturing	21.1	24.5	30.2	22.1	23.2	25.1	23.8	31.3
Other manufacturing	12.0	12.8	12.2	12.7	12.7	12.4	12.3	12.6
Mining	22.0	22.5	24.2	20.4	22.0	21.8	21.5	18.1
Other industry	10.4	10.7	9.7	10.9	10.9	10.8	11.0	10.2
B. Average annual growth rate, 2008-20								
Industrial growth rate		5.7	8.8	5.6	5.6	5.7	5.5	8.5
Construction		5.2	8.1	6.0	5.4	5.2	5.5	8.8
Manufacturing		6.1	10.2	5.1	5.6	6.0	5.5	9.7
Agriculture-related manufacturing		6.5	11.6	5.3	5.9	6.7	6.0	11.2
Other manufacturing		5.2	7.0	4.8	4.9	4.8	4.6	6.5
Mining		4.8	7.2	4.5	4.7	4.8	4.7	4.9
Other industry		7.5	9.6	7.4	7.5	7.4	7.5	9.5
C. Contribution to industrial growth, 2008-20 average								
Industrial growth contribution to GDP		30.9	44.5	25.9	33.3	28.9	26.5	33.8
Contribution to industrial GDP growth								
Construction		28.7	25.7	36.0	31.6	29.2	32.1	31.6
Manufacturing		38.3	44.6	32.2	35.1	38.3	35.1	45.3
Agriculture-related manufacturing		26.7	34.6	21.2	23.9	27.6	24.7	35.4
Other manufacturing		11.5	9.8	11.0	11.2	10.6	10.4	9.7
Mining		19.1	18.7	17.4	18.8	18.5	18.3	11.6
Other industry		13.9	10.9	14.3	14.4	14.0	14.5	11.6

Source: Authors, based on Ghana dynamic computable general equilibrium model results.
Note: GDP means gross domestic product.

Productivity-led growth improves the country's competitiveness in the manufacturing sector; the model results show that manufacturing exports grow more rapidly than the sector's production as a whole in Scenario 2. Total manufacturing and agriculture-related manufacturing exports grow, respectively, at 11.3 percent and 11.5 percent annually compared with 6.1 percent in the base-run scenario (Table 6.8). This results in a surge in the share of manufacturing exports in manufacturing production to 21.1 percent, with agriculture-related manufacturing exports as a share of agriculture-related manufacturing production increasing to 35.4 percent (see Table 6.5, Part A). Increased manufacturing production stimulates the demand for imported intermediates and capital goods, most of which are not produced domestically. Because of this, annual growth in manufacturing imports also increases, from 5.0 percent in the base run to 5.5 percent in this scenario. However, productivity-led growth helps the domestic agriculture-related manufacturing substitute for imports, because most of these goods are produced for domestic markets. The annual growth rate of agriculture-related manufacturing imports declines from 4.7 percent in the base run to 3.4 percent in this scenario (see Table 6.8). With import substitution in the agriculture-related manufacturing sector, the ratio of imports to domestic consumption of agriculture-related manufacturing products falls to 29.7 percent by 2020, down from 40.9 percent in 2007. For the manufacturing sector as a whole, however, imports still account for 52.6 percent of domestic consumption by 2020, only a slight decrease from 56.6 percent in 2007, driven by increased imports of capital goods to meet investment needs (see Table 6.5).

The surge in manufacturing exports significantly increases the sector's contribution to total export growth, yet it also reduces agricultural export growth. Rapid growth in the processing sectors increases their demand for raw materials (often agricultural goods) and hence reduces the availability of these primary agricultural products for direct export. Closer inspection shows that the increase in manufacturing exports is driven by growth in cocoa processing and wood products, which account for 24 percent and 57 percent of agriculture-related manufacturing exports in 2007, respectively. Growth in these sectors' exports leads to declines in the growth of cocoa and forestry exports, from 3.8 percent annually in the base run to 3.3 percent in Scenario 2 for cocoa and from 6.8 to 4.2 percent for forestry (see Table 6.8). Average annual growth in processed cocoa exports increases from 6.4 percent in the base run to 7.3 percent in this scenario and from 3.3 percent in the base run to 8.8 percent in this scenario for wood and wood product exports. As a consequence, some primary agricultural exports are replaced by exports of processed goods with greater value-added content. Other types of labor-intensive manufacturing that use agricultural goods as inputs also grow, such

Table 6.8   Annual growth in Ghana's exports and imports in model results (percent), 2008-20 average

Source of growth	Base run	Scenarios with growth in:					Middle-income country
		Industry	Services	Export agriculture	Staples	All agriculture	
Total exports	5.7	6.7	7.3	6.3	5.6	6.2	7.9
Agriculture	5.0	3.8	6.0	7.2	4.7	7.0	6.0
Cocoa	3.8	3.3	4.6	11.3	5.6	5.1	6.7
Forestry	6.8	4.2	8.1	8.1	6.2	7.5	4.7
Others	8.1	7.3	8.3	14.0	7.9	13.8	13.6
Nonagriculture	6.1	8.3	8.1	5.7	6.2	5.7	9.0
Mining	5.3	7.7	5.2	5.1	5.2	5.0	5.5
Manufacturing	6.1	11.3	5.6	5.1	6.7	5.4	11.7
Agriculture-related manufacturing	6.1	11.5	5.5	5.1	6.7	5.5	11.8
Services	7.6	6.0	14.3	7.1	7.5	7.1	12.1
Total imports	5.0	5.7	6.0	5.4	4.9	5.3	6.4
Agriculture	5.2	7.6	6.9	5.8	2.1	2.7	5.9
Rice	4.7	6.3	5.8	5.2	1.5	2.2	4.4
Poultry	6.5	7.1	8.1	6.8	6.5	6.8	8.7
Nonagriculture	5.0	5.5	5.9	5.4	5.1	5.5	6.5
Manufacturing	5.0	5.5	5.9	5.4	5.1	5.5	6.5
Agriculture-related manufacturing	4.7	3.4	5.9	5.2	4.7	5.2	4.5

Source: Authors, based on Ghana dynamic computable general equilibrium model results.

as meat and fish processing, textiles, clothing, and footwear. Compared with the base-run scenario, Scenario 2 shows the share of agricultural exports in total exports falling from 39.7 percent in 2007 to 27.7 percent by 2020, driven mainly by a slowdown in cocoa exports. Cocoa exports account for 25.7 percent of total exports in 2007 and fall to 16.8 percent by 2020 in this scenario (see Table 6.6, Part A). Under Scenario 2, Ghana experiences a relatively large structural change within the industrial sector. The share of manufacturing in industrial GDP rises from 33.2 percent in 2007 to 42.5 percent by 2020 (see Table 6.7, Part A). Led by the increasingly important role of the manufacturing sector in the economy, the overall economic structure changes, too. The share of industry in the overall economy increases from 30.5 percent of total GDP in 2007 to 33.2 percent by 2020. However, the resulting structural change is still modest compared with the historical experiences of the countries reviewed in Chapter 2. For example, in Indonesia and Malaysia, the two countries with initial manufacturing shares of GDP at the beginning of their transformation similar to Ghana's today, manufacturing's shares of total GDP increased 15 and 11 percentage points, respectively, during the countries' transformation periods (1974–95 for Indonesia and 1960–77 for Malaysia).

There are four main reasons that the rapid growth in industry simulated in the model, especially in manufacturing, does not result in a significant change in Ghana's economic structure compared with what we observed in the reference countries discussed in Chapter 2. First, the agricultural sector accounts for a relatively larger share in Ghana's economy than in those of most of the reference countries at the time they started to transform from low- to middle-income status. Because of the difference in Ghana's initial economic structure, relatively rapid growth in the agricultural sector seems to be a precondition for accelerated overall economic growth. Without agricultural growth, rapid growth in other sectors will not significantly increase per capita incomes in Ghana.

The second reason that industry's share increases only modestly in this scenario is that manufacturing growth is highly dependent on material inputs from the agricultural sector. Agriculture-related manufacturing, such as food, cocoa, and wood processing, accounts for more than 60 percent of Ghana's manufacturing industry. This implies that growth in these manufacturing sectors depends on growth in agriculture, which not only provides inputs to manufacturing production but also lowers the cost of inputs, especially if agricultural growth is driven by productivity increases. Textiles, clothing, and footwear also use agricultural raw materials as inputs but are considerably less dependent on agriculture because labor forms a much larger share of their production costs than do intermediate inputs. These sectors have played a key role in the rapid growth of the manufacturing industry in China and Vietnam. However, they are quite small in Ghana, accounting for 6 percent of total manufacturing output value. Therefore, even with more than 10 percent annual growth in production in these subsectors, their share in total manufacturing could not rise significantly under this scenario.

The third reason is related to demand constraints on certain food-processing products. Many such products are produced for domestic markets. Without additional growth in other sectors, especially in agriculture, the incomes of most rural households that depend on agriculture for their livelihoods cannot grow at a rate similar to that of the supply of processed foods. As a result, the prices of some food-processing products fall. Although this can benefit rural and urban households as consumers, it limits the growth potential of these sectors because their growth cannot deviate greatly from agricultural and other sectors' growth rates. The model includes two kinds of food-processing sectors, one of which includes informal or local foods and is located mainly in rural areas. This sector's growth is more constrained by rural income growth, for which the major source is agriculture. Accordingly, growth in informal food processing cannot depart too much from agricultural growth in total.

Finally, the mining sector plays a limited role in accelerating industrial growth. Under the base-run scenario, that sector grows around 4.8 percent on average each year. If we factor in the potential growth due to newly found oil resources, mining growth reaches 7.2 percent annually. Still, the contribution of this resource-driven growth to overall economic growth remains rather limited.

In summary, Scenario 2 underlines the importance of the manufacturing sector for accelerating growth in Ghana and helping the country reach MIC status. However, it also shows that the manufacturing sector's growth capacity is constrained by agricultural and rural income growth. Agriculture has to support manufacturing growth by providing cheap raw materials and increasing rural incomes to expand domestic market opportunities for nonagricultural goods. To speed up manufacturing growth rates significantly beyond agriculture's growth rates, the country will have to develop more export-oriented manufacturing. Those sectors should be less reliant on agricultural inputs, as are the labor-intensive manufacturing sectors that developed rapidly in China and Vietnam.

Scenario 3: The Role of the Service Sector in Structural Change

Almost all countries reviewed in Chapter 2 had strong manufacturing growth at the center of their structural transformations. However, the expansion of industry was often accompanied by growth in services. In China and Vietnam, for example, the increase in the contribution of services to GDP during the transformation periods mirrored the relative decline in agriculture's contribution. Moreover, the service sector in India has been a leading driver of economywide growth. Even during Malaysia's transformation period, when services did not grow as rapidly as agriculture and manufacturing, the large size of the service sector meant that its contribution to the economy was important for sustaining a high level of overall growth. Therefore, unlike Scenario 2, which focused on accelerating industrial growth, Scenario 3 shows how accelerated growth in Ghana's service sector can contribute to the country's achieving MIC status.

The service sector already forms a large part of the Ghanaian economy, accounting for more than one-third of total GDP. It is difficult to compare the service sectors of various countries given the diversity of the service sector's subsectors: public and private, traded and nontraded, technology intensive and unskilled labor intensive, and high and low value. In Ghana the government forms a large component of the service sector, accounting for one-third of the overall sector (Table 6.9, Part A). By contrast, export-oriented services, such as those provided by luxury hotels, restaurants, tourism, and finance, account for only 2.1 percent of service GDP. The remaining private services are domestic market oriented, such as trade, transport, communications, and business services. Although government administration is an important employer, it is generally not a productive sector and is unable to become a primary driver of structural transformation in any successful developing countries, as discussed in Chapter 2. Therefore, in Scenario 3 we did not increase the public sector, opting rather to focus on private-sector services, both export and domestic oriented. The private services account for 23 percent of total GDP in Ghana, which is more than manufacturing and construction together (see Table 4.1).

Although the service sector includes the more labor-intensive trade and transport sectors, it also includes some of Ghana's more capital-intensive sectors, such as finance and communications. Therefore, in Scenario 3 we model an increase in both productivity and capital accumulation. As in the previous scenario, additional capital growth is financed through increased foreign inflows. However, because the service sector as a whole is less capital intensive than industry, the increase in foreign-financed investment is smaller than what was assumed in the previous scenario. Together these assumptions cause service GDP growth to increase from 6.4 percent per year in the base run to 8.8 percent per year in this scenario (see Table 6.2, Part A), similar to the increase in industrial growth in the previous scenario. Total GDP growth rises from 5.6 percent in the base run to 6.4 percent per year in this scenario.

The service sector is expected to have strong growth linkages in the economy. Private services, especially trade and transport, are important sources of employment, responsible for one in five unskilled jobs in Ghana. Trade and transport services are important inputs for other sectors in the economy, accounting for 7.4 percent of the overall cost of their production. Service-related spending also comprises 13.8 percent of the average cost of investment. Finally, according to GLSS5 (GSS 2007), private services make up 12.1 percent of the average household's consumption basket, and households tend to spend a greater share of their incomes on private services as their incomes rise. Therefore, expanding growth in private services has a significant effect on economywide growth that is beyond the service sector itself.

The most important channel through which rapid growth in services affects non-service sectors is the lowering of the service prices following improvements in the service sector's productivity. The domestic service price index falls by an average of 2.7 percent per year. That lowers production costs for both agricultural and industrial sectors. However, growth in the export service sectors competes for resources with other sectors, particularly

Table 6.9 Structure of Ghana's services and its subsectors' contribution to service growth in model results (percent)

Measure, sector	Initial value in 2007	Base run	Scenarios with growth in:					Middle-income country
			Industry	Services	Export agriculture	Staples	All agriculture	
A. Structure of services, 2020								
Services' share in gross domestic product (GDP)	34.4	34.7	33.7	36.8	34.0	34.9	34.2	35.3
Share in service GDP								
Private	65.9	68.5	69.1	70.1	68.5	68.6	68.6	70.5
Export-oriented	2.1	2.3	2.0	3.3	2.2	2.3	2.2	2.6
Public	32.0	29.1	28.9	26.6	29.3	29.1	29.2	26.9
B. Average annual growth rate, 2008-20								
Total services		5.9	5.9	8.0	5.9	5.9	5.9	7.9
Private		6.7	6.8	10.0	6.7	6.8	6.7	9.8
Export-oriented		5.7	4.4	9.0	5.3	5.6	5.2	6.9
Public		5.8	5.7	5.6	5.8	5.8	5.8	5.5
C. Contribution to services growth, 2008-20 average								
Service growth contribution to GDP		39.3	33.2	48.8	36.8	37.3	35.1	38.6
Contribution to service GDP growth								
Private		70.6	71.5	78.4	70.6	70.9	70.8	78.9
Export-oriented		2.0	1.4	2.7	1.8	1.9	1.8	1.9
Public		27.5	27.1	18.9	27.5	27.2	27.4	19.2

Source: Authors, based on Ghana dynamic computable general equilibrium model results.

industrial sectors. This is partly due to the relatively stable prices of export services and may negatively affect growth in the other sectors. In total, the contribution of services to GDP growth increases from 39.8 percent in the base run to 49.5 percent in Scenario 3, while the service sector's share in GDP increases only modestly, from 34.7 percent in the base run to 36.8 percent in this scenario (see Table 6.2, Parts A and C).

So far we have emphasized the growth-linkage effects of private domestic-oriented services as the main reason that service-driven growth generates more economywide growth. Export services also contribute positively to faster overall growth. Export services generated 15.2 percent of Ghana's export earnings in 2007, and there is a potential to expand services further, such as tourism, hotel, and business services (see Table 6.6, Part A).

Under Scenario 3 we assumed that productivity in export-oriented services would increase such that the subsector's average growth rate would increase from 5.7 percent per year in the base run to 9.0 percent per year (see Table 6.9, Part B). Service exports would grow even more rapidly, accelerating from 7.6 percent to 14.3 percent per year (see Table 6.8). However, given the small initial size of this subsector in the economy, its contribution to total service growth is modest, rising from 2.0 percent in the base run to 2.7 percent in this scenario (see Table 6.9).

In summary, the service growth scenario clearly demonstrates the significant contribution of the service sector in helping Ghana achieve MIC status by 2020. Ghana undoubtedly has the potential to expand its export services, such as tourism and business services, and provide substitutes for imported services. However, this subsector is currently very small compared with domestic-oriented services. Thus, even if the growth rate of Ghana's export services were to match that of India's export services, it is unlikely that such growth in its current form could engender significant structural transformation. The benefits of service-sector growth are not limited to exports. The model demonstrates that greater economywide growth can be stimulated through expanding domestic services, especially in the trade and transport sectors. It is the strong growth linkages of the service sector that explain, at least in part, why countries such as China and Thailand have experienced more rapid service-sector growth alongside manufacturing-led transformations.

Scenario 4: Agricultural Growth and Poverty Reduction

Scenarios 2 and 3 show that growth acceleration in either industry or services alone is not sufficient to drive Ghana's per capita GDP to $1,000 by 2020. Growth led by the industrial and service sectors can increase per capita GDP by $100 each over the next 13 years. The literature and experiences from many countries, including Ghana (Chapters 2–4), suggest that agriculture can play an important role not only in accelerating growth, but also in reducing poverty as an important part of transformation. Given these multiple roles of agriculture, we go beyond the analyses of other sectors. In Scenarios 4a and 4b, we first focus on growth in agricultural exports and staple foods in sequence. We then assess the role of agriculture in poverty reduction via Green Revolution-type productivity growth and the sector's visible and invisible transfers to the rest of the economy using a method developed by Winters et al. (1998).

The Multiplier Effects of Staples-Led Growth Compared to Export-Led Growth

Export-led agricultural growth increases the rate of annual agricultural GDP growth to 5.5 percent, 0.9 percentage point higher than its base-run level (see Table 6.2, Part B). Production of exportable agricultural goods, including forestry goods, accounts for about 37 percent of agricultural GDP. In Scenario 4a we assume that there is little market constraint on the expansion of nontraditional exports, and hence exportable vegetables, fruits, and other nontraditional export crops grow at 12-14 percent annually, increasing from their base-run growth of 7-8 percent. Growth in traditional export crops, particularly cocoa, and in forestry products also increases, from 4-6 percent annually in the base run to 6-7 percent in this scenario. In total, the value added of export agriculture grows at 6.9 percent per year in this scenario, increasing from 4.3 percent in the base run. Despite such rapid growth, the relatively weak links of these export sectors with the rest of economy result in a limited overall growth impact. Total annual GDP growth increases to 5.8 percent, only 0.2 percentage point higher than growth in the base run (see Table 6.2, Part A). Thus, export-led growth alone will make only a small contribution to Ghana's achievement of MIC status. It will generate an additional $32 of per capita GDP over the base-run scenario's 2020 level of $838 (see Table 6.2, Part D).

We evaluate the growth contribution of staple crops and livestock production in Scenario 4b. About 63 percent of Ghana's agricultural GDP can be classified as arising from staple and livestock production, which includes cereals (9 percent of agricultural GDP), root crops (24 percent of agricultural GDP), and livestock (8 percent of agricultural GDP). The model also includes pulses and oilseed crops, which are both cash and staple crops in the country. Realistic and modest growth is assumed for the staple crops (except for rice) in the scenario given that income elasticity is generally low in consumer demand functions for them. For example, the value added of total root crops grows at 4.0 percent per year in the base run and increases to only 4.8 percent in this scenario. However, we assume much higher additional growth in rice and livestock products, given that these products are highly income elastic and the country has increasingly depended on imports to meet domestic demand for them. Driven by growth in rice and poultry, in this scenario cereals and livestock grow at 7.9 percent and 9.5 percent, respectively, whereas their growth rates are 4.7 percent and 6.7 percent in the base run.

With growth at the subsector level discussed earlier, the rate of annual agricultural GDP growth is 5.6 percent in this scenario, 1.0 percent higher than in the base run. This results in a rate of total GDP growth of 5.9 percent (see Table 6.2, Part A), and per capita GDP increases to $852 by 2020—$14 more than in the base run (see Table 6.2, Part D). An interesting question to further investigate is why staple-led growth generates more overall economic growth but less per capita income. The reason is the price effect. While GDP growth is measured in the real terms, per capita income is measured at current prices (in U.S. dollars), so changes in prices affect the outcome. To be able to compete in the international market and promote import substitution, productivity-led growth must lower domestic prices for import-competitive products. As shown in Table 6.5, imported rice accounts for 70 percent of domestic rice consumption, and import poultry accounts for 95.4 percent of consumption. Without improvements in productivity for these products, the ratio of imports to consumption further rises in the other scenarios discussed earlier. For example, in the case of industry-led growth, rice imports will increase to more than 78 percent of domestic consumption, and for poultry the ratio of imports to consumption will rise to 97 percent. With increased productivity in rice and poultry production in this scenario, the ratio of imports falls to 42.6 percent in the case of rice and 92.8 percent for poultry. Although lowering the domestic prices may indicate less growth in per capita incomes, it definitely benefits the poor, who spend a large portion of their incomes on food consumption.

The analysis in previous chapters indicates that the role of agriculture in economic transformation goes beyond growth and is also important for income distribution and poverty reduction. We therefore go beyond the analysis employed for the nonagricultural sectors discussed earlier and examine two additional dimensions. First we measure the transfers from agriculture to the rest of the economy. This analysis is particularly important for the agricultural sector, because public investments and the involvement of the public sector in general have played important roles in agricultural growth in the successfully transforming countries. Then we assess the distributional and poverty impacts of agricultural growth across subnational regions and household groups.

To achieve this, we consider the whole agriculture sector in Scenario 4c, which represents a combination of Scenarios 4a and 4b in which exogenous

increases in productivity across all agricultural subsectors are the forces driving overall growth. On the other hand, land expansion remains the same as
in the base run. The productivity growth rates for crop sectors are chosen to
target achievable yields at the zonal level and are consistent with the gap
between current and achievable yields within each zone.[2] Under this scenario, Ghana's agricultural sector will grow at an average annual rate of 6.3
percent over the next 13 years.

Promoting Productivity-Led Growth by Closing Existing Yield Gaps

Under the Green Revolution-type agricultural growth represented by Scenario 4c, growth accelerates in all subsectors, and productivity improvement
rather than land expansion is the main contributor to growth. At the crop
level, productivity growth becomes the dominant factor in the output growth
of maize, sorghum, cassava, and yams, contributing 50–75 percent of output
growth in these crops (Table 6.10).

The Contribution to Transformation of Agriculture's Invisible Transfers

The experiences of Asian countries show that unleashing a Green Revolution
has often required massive public investments, raising the question of the
cost of such growth acceleration. Although financing productivity growth is
beyond the scope of this monograph, it is necessary to understand the benefit
of a Green Revolution type of agricultural growth measured monetarily. Such
measurement of agriculture's contribution to economywide growth is not only
helpful in better understanding the role of agriculture but can also provide
powerful arguments for developing and implementing pro-agriculture policies
and increasing agricultural investments. Here the agricultural sector's contribution to the economy is measured as a surplus transferred from agriculture
to nonagriculture. This definition is based on the insights of development
economists in the 1950s and 1960s, who characterized the dynamics of the
economic development process as a dual system (see Chapter 2). According
to this theory, agriculture supports the rest of the economy by transferring
a surplus from agriculture to nonagriculture. Some of these transfers are visible, that is, they can be directly observed. Visible transfers are often those
that can be observed from a country's statistics, such as its agricultural trade

---

[2] In the CGE model producers in crop sectors (much as in the other production sectors) choose
inputs (such as land, labor, capital, and a set of intermediate inputs) simultaneously to maxi-
mize their profits using a given technology. Because both outputs and inputs (including land)
are endogenous variables in the model, it is impossible to directly target crop yield levels exogenously. Thus, TFP is an exogenous variable in the CGE model's production functions, and the
exogenous "shock" to this parameter in the simulation is imposed in order to target specific
yield levels.

Table 6.10   Productivity contribution to Ghana's crop growth in the agricultural growth scenario (percent), 2008-20 average

Crop	Annual growth rate under agriculture scenario			Additional yield growth from base run	Land	Yield
	Output	Land	Yield			
Maize	7.3	3.3	3.8	1.1	45.6	54.4
Rice	10.6	6.3	4.1	1.0	58.8	41.2
Sorghum	5.9	2.9	3.0	0.9	48.5	51.5
Cassava	4.8	1.2	3.6	1.0	24.7	75.3
Yams	5.0	1.3	3.7	1.0	25.9	74.1
Cocoyams	4.7	1.3	3.4	0.8	26.9	73.1
Cowpeas	5.0	1.4	3.6	1.3	28.0	72.0
Soybeans	8.1	4.7	3.3	1.1	57.3	42.7
Oil palm	5.9	2.2	3.6	0.8	37.9	62.1
Groundnuts	6.2	2.1	4.0	1.2	33.7	66.3
Other nuts	6.5	2.8	3.6	0.7	42.9	57.1
Fruits (domestic)	5.8	1.8	3.9	1.1	31.6	68.4
Fruits (export)	13.5	9.0	4.1	0.6	66.6	33.4
Vegetables (domestic)	5.2	1.4	3.8	1.3	26.3	73.7
Vegetables (export)	12.4	8.0	4.0	0.5	64.7	35.3
Bananas	4.9	1.3	3.6	0.5	25.9	74.1
Cocoa	6.2	3.6	2.5	0.3	57.8	42.2
Other crops	6.8	3.2	3.4	0.8	47.8	52.2
Other export crops	11.7	7.6	3.8	0.7	65.2	34.8

Source: Authors, based on Ghana dynamic computable general equilibrium model results.

surplus, which is often a main provider of the foreign exchange needed to finance imported capital and the intermediate goods used by nonagricultural sectors. However, the majority of the surpluses transferred from agriculture to nonagriculture are often invisible and not recorded in country statistics. An important invisible transfer stems from decreases in domestic agricultural prices, which often result from improved agricultural productivity. The invisible nature of these transfers has frequently led to underestimation of the role of agriculture in economic development. As a consequence, the policy and investment priorities of governments have typically focused on promoting agricultural exports to generate visible surpluses.

Here we apply a method developed by Winters et al. (1998) to quantitatively measure the monetary benefits that account for both visible and invisible transfers of agriculture to the nonagricultural economy. Based on the model results of the agricultural growth scenario (4c), to assess surplus transfers under this scenario we first disaggregate increased market demand for agricultural goods as consumer goods, intermediate goods, and investment goods.

In financial terms (measured in millions of new cedi),[3] the total financial transfer out of agriculture amounts to about 1,758 million cedi over the 13 years between 2008 and 2020, equivalent to 17.7 percent of the increased total GDP over the same period. In 2020 alone, the transfer will be equivalent to 1.5 percent of total GDP in this specific year (Table 6.11). However, the visible transfer in this period is actually negative. This transfer includes the net value of increased demand for agricultural goods by the nonagricultural sector and for nonagricultural goods by the agricultural sector (which is negative) in the domestic market and the agricultural trade surplus (which is positive; see Table 6.11). With 7,682 million cedi of accumulated agricultural trade surpluses over the 13 years, the visible transfer through foreign markets is huge. However, the transfer in the domestic market as the net value of increased demand for agricultural goods and for nonagricultural goods is negative and substantial (-8,379 million cedi over the 13 years), which leads to an overall negative total visible transfer out of agriculture.

The invisible transfer out of agriculture can be broken down into three parts: the transfer through lowered agricultural prices, that through increased nonagricultural prices, and that through increased returns to factors employed in the agricultural sectors. In total, the net invisible transfer from agriculture is 2,455 million cedi over the 13 years and 514 million in 2020 alone. Lowering agricultural prices results in a transfer of 1,459 million cedi out of the agricultural sector, while increased nonagricultural prices contribute modestly as the invisible transfer (487 million cedi during 2008-20). Because the factors move into agriculture, the transfer constitutes a positive invisible transfer because agriculture has to pay a higher price for the increased factor employment (509 million cedi during 2008-20).

We further evaluate the monetary value of the net physical flows in the forms of products and factors. For the products we break down the contribution into domestic and foreign markets, while we disaggregate the factor contribution according to the three subsectors it employs, that is, staples, import-substitutable agriculture, and export agriculture. The contribution of production is positive, mainly due to the increased agricultural trade surplus (visible transfer), while the factor contribution is negative because more factors are employed in agriculture under the agricultural growth scenario.

By distinguishing factor employment in either export or staple agriculture we can further evaluate the different roles of these two agricultural subsectors in economic development. Productivity growth in staple agriculture implies that a country can produce more food and agricultural materials using

---

[3] One new Ghana cedi is worth about US$0.94.

Table 6.11   Visible and invisible transfers of a financial surplus from agriculture in Ghana under the agricultural growth scenario

Transfer	Million cedi, accumulated in 2008-20	As a percentage of increases in GDP accumulated in 2008-20	Million cedi, 2020	As a percentage of GDP, 2020
Financial transfer out of agriculture	1,758	17.7	395	1.50
Net visible transfer from agriculture	-697	-7.0	-120	-0.45
Through domestic market	-8,379	-84.3	-1,436	-5.46
Through foreign trade	7,682	77.3	1,316	5.01
Net invisible transfer from agriculture	2,455	24.7	514	1.96
Through lowered agricultural prices	1,459	14.7	300	1.14
Through increased nonagricultural prices	487	4.9	101	0.39
Through increased factor prices	509	5.1	113	0.43
Corresponding monetary value of net physical flows out of agriculture	5,555	55.9	435	1.66
Product contribution	6,000	60.3	524	2.35
Net transfer through domestic markets	-1,683	-16.9	-349	-1.33
Net transfer through foreign markets	7,682	77.3	874	3.32
Factor contribution	-444	-4.5	-89	-0.34
From staples	81	0.8	16	0.06
From import substitutable	-145	-1.5	-28	-0.11
From export agriculture	-406	-4.1	-82	-0.31

Source: Authors, based on Ghana dynamic computable general equilibrium model results.
Note: GDP means gross domestic product.

less labor input. This further lowers the cost of labor and allows labor to migrate from staple agriculture to other economic activities, such as those in the rural nonfarm or urban sectors, and hence to engage in nonagricultural growth. As shown in Table 6.11, the factor contribution of staples is positive (that is, the factor is moving out of staple production), with 81 million in total between 2008 and 2020 in the scenario. This result is consistent with what has been observed in many Asian countries during their development process, that is, the supply of low-cost food and more labor moving out of agriculture are critical to support the development of labor-intensive manufacturing and services.

On the other hand, the factor contribution through export agriculture is negative (that is, more of the factor is employed in export agricultural production) at -406 million cedi for the same period. Surplus transfers of export agriculture are often highly visible and help to provide foreign exchange earnings to the nonagricultural sector for importing capital goods and inter-mediates; hence, export agriculture has played an important role in development. However, without productivity growth in staple agriculture, growth in export agriculture can increase the demand for food, which can result in either higher food prices in domestic markets or the need for more food imports. Also, increased demand for labor and capital to support growth in export agriculture can inflate factor prices. Under these conditions, it often becomes difficult to develop labor-intensive manufacturing and services, and such a situation could significantly slow structural transformation.

Regional Impacts of Agricultural Growth

Regional differences in agricultural growth remain under the agriculture scenario, but the growth gap becomes smaller compared to the base run (Table 6.12, column 1). The combination of agricultural production activities differs substantially among the four agroecological zones, and land productivity improves differentially among the crops under this scenario. For example, at the national level the rate of additional yield growth is as high as 3.6 percent for cassava and 3.7 percent for yams (see Table 6.10, column 4). However, because root crops account for only 8.4 percent of the Coast Zone's agricultural value added, this high rate of growth in root crops has a relatively small impact on the zone's agricultural growth under this scenario (Table 6.13).

As a result of differences in agroecological conditions, the sources of growth in the agriculture scenario are quite different across the four zones. Although productivity is the most important factor in explaining regional agricultural growth in this scenario, the contribution of land expansion still accounts for more than 50 percent of agricultural growth in the Northern Savannah (see Table 6.12). On the other hand, land continues to be the smallest factor in agricultural growth in the Coast Zone, accounting for only 14.1 percent of zonal agricultural growth in this scenario.

Table 6.12   Agricultural growth in Ghana across zones under the agricultural growth scenario (percent), 2008-20

Zone	Agricultural gross domestic product annual growth	Additional growth from base run	Contribution to agricultural growth (%)			
			Land	Labor	Capital	Total factor productivity
Coastal	6.9	2.2	14.1	20.3	6.6	59.0
Forest	6.3	1.8	32.5	18.1	10.8	38.6
Southern Savannah	5.7	1.4	22.8	11.4	9.3	56.4
Northern Savannah	6.9	1.6	50.6	16.9	9.2	23.3
Nation	6.3	1.7	24.1	11.8	6.8	57.3

Source: Authors, based on Ghana dynamic computable general equilibrium model results.

Table 6.13   Additional subsector growth in Ghana across the four zones under the agricultural growth scenario (percent), 2008-20

Subsector	Coastal	Forest	Southern Savannah	Northern Savannah
A. Additional annual growth from base run				
Cereals	3.9	4.5	2.8	2.9
Root crops	1.1	1.2	1.0	0.8
Other staple crops	1.6	1.8	1.1	1.3
Export crops	4.4	2.4	1.1	1.3
Livestock	1.9	1.8	2.0	2.4
Fishery and forestry	0.8	0.5	0.5	0.6
B. Contribution to additional agricultural gross domestic product growth from base run				
Cereals	21.4	15.5	17.5	29.7
Root crops	4.3	11.9	26.9	18.0
Other staple crops	15.5	17.5	21.3	28.2
Export crops	36.2	41.9	17.5	0.7
Livestock	9.3	7.4	8.2	22.8
Fishery and forestry	13.2	5.7	8.6	0.7

Source: Authors, based on Ghana dynamic computable general equilibrium model results.

The contribution of various subsectors to regional agricultural growth also differs across zones in this scenario. As shown in Table 6.13 (Part B), export crops contribute the most to additional agricultural growth in the Coast and Forest Zones. In the Southern Savannah, the contribution of root crops is the highest, though other staples also play important roles. In the Northern Savannah, additional growth in agriculture comes mainly from cereals and other staple crop groups, while export crops play an insignificant role in this zone.

The Continuing High Level of Poverty in the North

Accelerating agricultural growth and its spillover effects on nonagricultural sectors also accelerates poverty reduction. Our model results suggest that both the national and rural poverty rates of Ghana will be halved one year earlier under the agricultural scenario than under the base run. By 2015 the national poverty rate will fall to 12.5 percent under the agricultural scenario compared to 16.4 in the base run. The rural poverty rate will fall to 17.5 percent by 2015, substantially lower than the 23.2 percent under the base run. This translates into an additional 850,000 people (mostly from rural areas) moving out of poverty by 2015 under the agricultural scenario (Table 6.14).

The model results show that poverty reduction is the result of increased incomes and lowered food prices driven by productivity growth in the agricultural sector. Thus urban households share the gains from agricultural growth

Table 6.14   Poverty reduction in Ghana under the agricultural
growth scenario

Area	Data, 2005	Base run, 2015	Agricultural growth scenario, 2015	Additional poverty reduction by 2015
North	62.7	48.6	40.6	7.9
Rest of the country	19.7	8.6	5.6	2.9
National	28.5	16.4	12.5	3.9
Rural	39.2	23.2	17.5	5.7

Source: Authors, based on Ghana dynamic computable general equilibrium model results.

acceleration, with rural and urban incomes growing at similar rates; sector linkages and price effects mean that the income growth rate is similar for urban and rural households (Table 6.15). However, rural households benefit more than urban households in terms of additional income growth (0.25 vs. 0.45 percent, respectively; see Table 6.15). Among the urban household groups, those in the two savannah zones are the major beneficiaries from agricultural growth. Annual incomes increase by 5.59 percent for these two household groups, and the additional income growth is the highest for these two groups of households (see Table 6.15). Growth in total income for the rural households is led by the more rapid increases in agricultural income. As shown in Table 6.15, agricultural income grows more rapidly than total income except in the Southern Savannah Zone, and additional agricultural income growth is greater than total income growth for all zones.

The relatively high rate of income growth for rural Northern Savannah households suggests that poverty reduction in the north might speed up. As shown in Table 6.14, the additional poverty reduction in 2015 under this scenario is 7.9 percentage points in the north versus 5.7 percent for rural households nationally, and 3.9 percent for the nation as a whole. However, given the high initial poverty rate in the north, the poverty rate in this region will remain at a high level of 40.6 percent in 2015, increasing the gap between poverty levels in the north versus the rest of the country and further exacerbating regional divergence.

It is important to emphasize the need for further poverty reduction in the Northern Savannah, but this discussion has often concentrated on a single poverty line. In order to better understand the challenge of reducing poverty in the north and design more appropriate policies, an analysis should go beyond the poverty line definition in order to help us better understand the size and nature of this challenge. Cross-country empirical studies show that

Table 6.15   Growth in household income in Ghana under the agricultural scenario, 2008-20

Area	Agricultural income		Total income	
	Annual growth under agricultural scenario	Additional growth from base run	Annual growth under agricultural scenario	Additional growth from base run
Urban			5.53	0.25
Accra			5.46	0.25
Coastal			5.59	0.25
Forest			5.63	0.23
Southern Savannah			5.59	0.28
Northern Savannah			5.59	0.29
Rural	5.79	0.87	5.50	0.45
Coastal	6.21	1.61	5.66	0.59
Forest	5.94	1.30	5.48	0.65
Southern Savannah	5.31	0.56	5.36	0.26
Northern Savannah	5.99	0.23	5.72	0.22

Source: Authors, based on Ghana dynamic computable general equilibrium model results.

the elasticity of poverty reduction to income growth is lower for groups with initially low per capita income (Easterly 2007). This finding is supported by the case of poverty reduction in Ghana. We use per capita expenditure data from GLSS5 (GSS 2007) to illustrate this argument. The two graphs included in Figure 6.1 depict the population distribution of those in poverty in rural areas of the Northern Savannah and elsewhere in the country. The rural population under the nationally defined poverty line of 90 new cedi (at 1999 prices, roughly $90) is equal to 100 in each region in the graphs. The black line in each graph shows the population distribution ranking from poor to less poor according to per capita income. If the 6 percent annual agricultural GDP growth were shared equally by all rural households in the country, it would be roughly equal to a 40 percent total increase in per capita incomes for all households (assuming that the population growth rate is 2.5 percent annually). With this equally distributed growth, households with per capita incomes of between 65 and 90 new cedi in GLSS5 would be lifted above the poverty line. The dashed line in each graph shows the share of the population that would stay below the poverty line even after their incomes had increased by 40 percent. Because the incomes of almost two-thirds of the poor in rural households outside the Northern Savannah range between 65 and 90 new cedi in GLSS5, the poverty rate among these rural households would fall to 8 per-cent, a significant drop from the initial 20 percent. In sharp contrast, only 20

Figure 6.1   Population distribution under the poverty line in rural areas of Ghana, 2007

a. The poor with per capita income less than 90 cedi, non-Northern Savannah

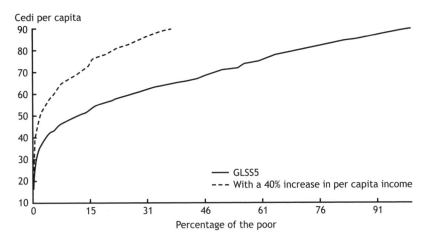

b. The poor with per capita income less than 90 cedi, Northern Savannah

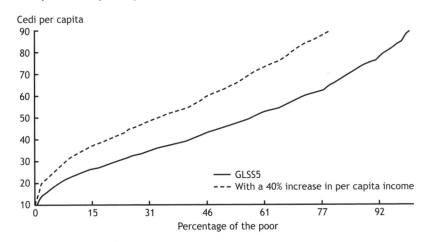

Source: Authors' calculation using Ghana Living Standard Survey Round 5 (GLSS5) (GSS 2007).
Note: One new Ghana cedi is worth about US$0.94.

percent of the rural poor in the Northern Savannah earned incomes between 65 and 90 new cedi as reported in GLSS5 (GSS 2007). Applying the same 40 percent income increase per capita to this group would therefore lead to significantly lower poverty reduction in the north, where the rural poverty rate would only fall to 53 percent from its initial level of 68 percent.

These results emphasize the special attention that should be paid to people whose incomes are far below the poverty line, that is, the segment of the population that can be classified as extremely poor. Obviously rapid income growth will not be sufficient to lift the poorest of the poor out of poverty, indicating that more targeted policies and investments are urgently needed. Thus, although halving the poverty rate between 1990 and 2008 will connote a great success for Ghana, the continued fight against poverty in this country will have to increasingly concentrate on the poorest of the poor, most of whom live in the Northern Savannah Zone.

Scenario 5: Broad-Based Growth in Transformation

Results from the previous analysis in this chapter show that rapid growth in one sector alone will not lead to a significant increase in per capita income. Therefore, combined growth across sectors will be necessary for Ghana to double incomes in the next 10-15 years. In Scenario 5 we combined the labor, land, capital, and productivity growth assumptions we applied in the previous three scenarios (Scenarios 2, 3, and 4) to evaluate the joint impact of accelerated growth for the economy as a whole. This scenario shows each sector's GDP growth rate accelerating through enhanced intersector linkage effects, with agriculture growing at 6.1 percent, industry at 8.5 percent, and services at 8.6 percent (see Table 6.2, Part A).

With this combined growth acceleration in all sectors, total GDP growth rises to 7.7 percent per year, and the rate of annual per capita GDP growth is 5.36 percent. With such growth, Ghana will reach its goal of achieving MIC status, and its per capita income will be $1,041 by 2020, almost doubling the $587 of 2007 (see Table 6.2, Part D).

In Scenario 5, productivity growth is the driving force in Ghana's reaching MIC status, supported by capital accumulation, which causes labor's contributions to growth to decrease. Productivity's contribution rises by more than 10 percentage points (see Table 6.3). Accelerated growth is also supported by capital accumulation, and a relatively stable ratio of investment to GDP indicates that investment must grow at a speed similar to that of the economy (see Table 6.4). Although investments continue to be financed by domestic sources, the share of government investment (including foreign grants and foreign aid channeled through the government) as the major financial source rises.

Structural change, in terms of sectoral composition, remains limited, despite differing growth rates across sectors. Although the annual growth rate of agriculture is the lowest among the three sectors and is about 2.5 percentage points lower than the growth rates of the other two nonagricultural sectors, agriculture's share of total GDP remains 34 percent (only 1.1 percentage point less than the share in 2007). With 8.5 percent annual growth, the industrial sector's share in GDP remains constant and rises slightly, from 30.5 percent in 2007 to 30.7 percent by 2020. Although the service sector's growth rate is the highest, the sector's share of GDP increases by only 1 percentage point, from 34.4 percent in 2007 to 35.4 percent in 2020. This "inconsistency" between the sector's contribution to GDP growth and its share in GDP is the result of changes in the relative prices. Compared with the GDP deflator, agricultural prices rise and industrial and domestic service price indexes fall, which causes the share of agriculture in GDP, measured in current prices, to remain constant while industrial and service shares of GDP do not increase much.

These results from the model conclude the analytical part of this monograph. The final chapter summarizes the main findings and draws lessons for future transformation policies, particularly in Ghana.

CHAPTER 7

Conclusions and Principal Messages

There are few examples of successfully transforming countries in Africa. To understand opportunities for and challenges to achieving rapid transformation and to examine how transformation in Africa might differ from that in other regions, this monograph has taken a two-step approach. We first provided a literature review on economic transformation and a descriptive analysis by combining broad lessons from selected successfully transforming countries and lessons from Ghana's own economic history. Based on this analysis, we then developed a highly disaggregated DCGE model to assess Ghana's growth options in the transformation process with special attention to the role of agriculture and Green Revolution–type growth. With this approach, the monograph has addressed the following questions: (1) What can Ghana learn from transformation theory and other countries' successful transformation experiences? (2) What lessons does Ghana's own economic history provide for the country's future transformation and design of development strategies? (3) Given Ghana's progress in institutional development and macroeconomic stability and its current socioeconomic structure, what are the country's broad options to accelerate growth and transformation? (4) What role will the agricultural sector play in Ghana's economic transformation? Is productivity-led agricultural growth feasible, and what are its potential impacts? (5) What are the implications of these results for development strategies in Ghana? Based on the analysis conducted in Chapters 2–6, we identify a set of strategic policy implications as a summary of the monograph.

The monograph has emphasized the importance of private-sector-led productivity growth across all economic sectors in the process of transformation. To actively support this process, government policies and public investments are important conditions for success. The following discussion identifies important areas for policy change, institutional reform, and public investments. Government interventions that entail policy and institutional reforms, such as improvements in legislation, regulations, and rules, usually come at low financial cost and with few budget implications. Interventions based on public investment require additional funds, changes in the composition of existing budgets, and/or improvements in the spending efficiency. Obviously the amount of public investment required to reach Ghana's goal of rapid economic transformation in the next 10-15 years is large. Given the strong commitment of the international community in recent years, and the newly discovered oil, we argue that resources will be available to finance the necessary productivity-enhancing public investments.[1] Preconditions for the successful use of these fresh funds are that public investments be well planned and targeted based on evidence, that processes be transparent and well monitored, and that potential outcomes be assessed in advance and properly evaluated throughout the process.

The principal messages that have emerged from our study can be seen in terms of seven priorities, for each of which detailed suggestions for policy action and areas for further research are now provided.

1. It Is Necessary to Move from Vision to Action

This monograph emphasizes that vision is essential, goals need to be realistic, and the approaches must be appropriate. In the past, governments in Ghana have often been too ambitious and unfocused in pursuing their goals, and there has often been a "rush to claim success." The approaches adopted, such as state-led industrialization, were inappropriate given the endowments, although at the time import substitution was an acceptable aspect of post-independence nation-building. Much time has been lost in reversing these policies, partly because of the political instability that prevailed in the country.

In recent years, however, Ghana has made significant progress in improving the process of designing development strategies. Participation and consultation with stakeholders have become commonplace and accepted aspects

---

[1] Ghana has been identified as one of the few pilot countries in West Africa that is expected to receive large additional amounts of multidonor financial support through G20 commitments.

In 2007 oil was discovered off the coast of Ghana, with the total reserves estimated at between 500 million and 1.5 billion barrels and the potential for future government revenues estimated at US$1.0–1.5 billion annually (Osei and Domfe 2008; World Bank and IMF 2009). Measured by a modest long-term oil price of US$60 per barrel over the next 20 years, oil revenues will add around 30 percent to the government's income annually and constitute 10 percent of Ghana's GDP over the exploitation period.

As discussed in Chapter 5, where the CGE model is introduced, productivity growth in the model simulation is an exogenous process, and there is no endogenous link between productivity growth and public investment, though the government is included in the model as an economic agent. Thus we did not consider the additional revenues of oil inflows and additional foreign financial support for public investment in the model. By ignoring such activities in the model, we also ignore their general equilibrium effect on domestic prices and hence the resource allocation responses to these price changes. However, our assumption that inflows are the primary source of additional public investment to support productivity growth does not alter the implications of the CGE model results discussed in this monograph.

of strategic decisionmaking. Development strategy documents prepared in recent years, such as the Ghana Poverty Reduction Strategy, the agricultural sector framework, and the Food and Agriculture Sector Development Policy, were developed through extensive consultation (Kolavalli et al. 2010). Although participation has become part of the decisionmaking processes, policy interventions that entail specific actions to realize the objectives included in a strategy and that have effects on the ground require much more than a participatory process. One recent example for moving from strategy to implementation is Ghana's Savannah Accelerated Development Authority plan, which includes a set of concrete actions required to close the country's North–South gap. Obviously making policies evidence based and effectively implementing those policies are still two of the greatest challenges the Government of Ghana faces.

Policy consistency has significantly improved, and few cases of policy reversals have occurred following the structural adjustment period. Yet policy objectives often remain just statements, and policy implementation processes and outcomes are not sufficiently transparent and often without effective follow-up, including a lack of monitoring and evaluation. Thus, moving economic transformation from a strategic objective to a series of concrete policy actions is a key challenge facing the government. Indeed, the experiences of successfully transforming countries in Asia and Latin America have shown the importance of a committed government in implementing its development strategy. Economic transformation requires changes in the way governments work, and the development of a more outcome-oriented government with a stronger focus on development impacts will require substantial reforms and capacity-building within Ghana's government and administration.

2. Reforms That Go beyond Macroeconomic Stability and Stimulate the Dynamic Forces behind the Growth Process Are Critical

Political, institutional, and macroeconomic stability are necessary conditions for economic transformation. In Ghana, decades of political instability possibly delayed a shift away from state-led industrialization strategies and damaged an independent and capable civil service. Ambitious but inefficient investments in infrastructure and capital-intensive industrialization contributed to a rapid increase in macroeconomic imbalances and a vicious circle of policies detrimental to modernization. In recent years, major indicators of governance, political freedom, and fairness of elections have improved significantly in Ghana. Macroeconomic stability has finally been achieved since the implementation of the structural change programs in the late 1980s. The confidence in the country's creditworthiness and the prospects for both private and public investments are promising. Ghana is no longer seen as a country "where investment may prosper under one regime at best, but could not be guaranteed under the next one."

A stable democratic political system and macroeconomic stability are necessary conditions for Ghana's future growth, but they are not sufficient conditions for accelerating the growth and transformation process. This monograph shows that increasing productivity across all sectors will be the key to rapid transformation. A stabilized and liberalized macroeconomic environment has provided incentives to the private sector to invest in human and physical capital—the foundation of productivity changes—yet macroeconomic stability does not necessarily translate into a unique set of policy actions to stimulate the dynamic forces that lie behind the growth process (World Bank 2005b). Success stories from Asian and Latin American countries indicate that growth-enhancing policies and the ways governments are active in promoting growth differ across countries. Therefore, identifying country-specific binding constraints and the changes of binding constraints over time should be an integral part of the policymaking process (Rodrik 2007).

3. Attracting Foreign Direct Investment in Nonmineral Sectors Is Important

FDI plays an important role in productivity growth and economic structural change. The role of foreign investment in development goes beyond filling the investment gap and providing physical capital for growth. Foreign investment comes with new technology and fresh market opportunities, thus providing opportunities to create a more productive labor force and enhance management skills.[2] Indeed, Ghana's government has put a lot of effort into attracting foreign investment, and the list of advertised investment opportunities is long (TradeInvest Africa 2010). However, FDI inflows have largely been concentrated in the mineral sectors (gold and oil), sectors with fewer linkages with the rest of economy and relatively low spillover effects in technology and labor productivity.

Many factors have constrained FDI into sectors other than gold and oil, and a recent survey among investors helps identify key constraints that hold firms back from investing in nonmineral sectors in Ghana. The most important concerns for firms are mostly related to bureaucratic procedures and institutional barriers. Access to land, registration of property, and dealing with licenses are among the top constraints. To attract more FDI, Ghana thus needs to improve its investment climate, especially speeding up land admin-

---

[2] See Markusen (2002), Navaretti and Venables (2004), and Helpman (2006) for extensive literature reviews.

istration and property registration procedures to provide firms with security for their land and other property rights (Barthel, Busse, and Osei 2008).

The availability of skilled workers, labor productivity, and the cost of labor are also among the top concerns of foreign investors (Barthel, Busse, and Osei 2008). Here the government can play an important role through improvements of the current education system and policies related to education. More specifically, technical and managerial skills can be strengthened by improving vocational training and its links to academia, enhancing the capacity of the private sector to provide training for its workers, and linking the funding of training activities to outcomes and performance (World Bank 2007b). Fostering closer collaboration among institutions, such as the Ghana Investment Promotion Center and the labor unions, will also be important for maximizing the developmental benefits of FDI (Barthel, Busse, and Osei 2008).

When evidence from surveys of the business climate (focused on domestic firms) is added, access to electricity emerges as a top additional concern (World Bank 2007b). Improving access to electricity will require the scaling-up of investments in the sector to increase supply. Yet the efficiency of current electricity supply can also be significantly improved by budget-neutral measures such as reforms of the electricity distribution system, tariff and subsidy reform, and more efficient management and regulatory frameworks governing supply and demand (World Bank 2007b). Which of these factors are the most binding constraints and how to relax these constraints deserves more in-depth study in order to inform policy actions to attract foreign investment. Case studies of successful countries in other African and Asian countries will also prove useful.

Foreign investment that concentrates in sectors and projects with high spillover effects should be preferred, because this type of FDI is more likely to spur technological transfer and productivity growth through the adoption of innovations, learning by doing, management know-how, and training of the labor force. Examples of such sectors include textile industries in East and Southeast Asia and export services in India (Kikushi 1998; Ohno and Jirapatpimol 1998; Dutz 2007). On the contrary, FDI that creates enclave economies that are disconnected from local technology and markets have limited effects on productivity (Emerson 1982; Auty 1993). Factors related to such disconnection are often associated with the government's bias toward capital-intensive, large-scale foreign companies that tend to create little demand for local labor and inputs. With newly found oil the government has started to plan investments in various oil-processing industries and an aluminum smelter, in which large-scale foreign companies are the major partners and investors. This type of FDI will lead to rapid growth in Ghana's industrial sector and help the country achieve its MIC status goal sooner than expected.

Yet this type of FDI may do little to improve the productivity growth of labor and other factors in the rest of the economy. In providing support to facilitate FDI inflows government should thus pay more attention to sectors with high spillover effects and sectors that encourage the creation of industrial clusters and more jobs.

4. Small and Medium-Sized Manufacturing Enterprises Are Key to Broad-Based Transformation

In other countries the transformation process has often been led by manufacturing growth. The model simulation exercise in this monograph shows that Ghana also needs to accelerate its manufacturing sector's growth if it aims to double its 2005 per capita income over a period of 10–15 years. However, we find that the initial contribution of manufacturing in Ghana is likely to limit the sector's role in transformation. Simulations show that the current structure of Ghana's manufacturing sector is agriculture focused, which may constrain manufacturing's future growth capacity due to supply constraints from agriculture and demand constraints from rural households. On the other hand, agricultural growth acceleration can help overcome these constraints and trigger strong multiplier effects and growth in both the agricultural and the manufacturing sectors. Under this scenario, the experience of structural change in Ghana will possibly differ from that of other countries. The share of the manufacturing sector in the economy may not increase as rapidly as elsewhere, and accelerating growth in manufacturing (beyond the levels of agriculture) will mainly have to come from productivity changes and improved international competitiveness.

The size of the domestic market and fierce international competition may limit Ghana to developing certain types of manufacturing that are large scale in nature. Yet opportunities exist for developing small-scale manufacturing products and those oriented to the domestic market. Currently many of the low-cost consumer products demanded by the majority of Ghanaians are imported, mainly from Asia. Development of better-targeted domestic manufacturing products with competitive prices should be a policy priority to promote domestic manufacturing growth. Moreover, opportunities also exist related to imported manufacturing goods, which often create new demand for the production of parts (for example, the automobile assembly and repair cluster in Kumasi).

Experience from Asian countries has shown that small and medium-sized enterprises (SMEs) in the manufacturing and service sectors that are more "homegrown" are likely to be more consistent with a country's initial conditions and able to exploit the country's comparative advantages. The production of SMEs is not only more labor intensive but also more productive per unit of scarce capital, and hence it can generate more broad-based growth and transformation (Chuta and Liedholm 1979; Kilby and Liedholm 1986). This type of transformation has proven successful at early stages of transformation in China, Japan, the Philippines, and Thailand. In Japan, the networks of traditional putting-out relationships in the textile sector have often become nurseries for modern technology firms (Itoh and Tanimoto 1998). The establishment of rural garment factories and the strengthening of contractual relationships between rural and urban enterprises has been a driver of transformation in Thailand and the Philippines (Kikushi 1998; Ohno and Jirapatpimol 1998). Rural township enterprises in China often started as labor-intensive activities with low capital and technology requirements that produced products for rural and small-town markets. Given the low initial capital requirements, such enterprises can be established in many places and operated at different scales. In the process of creative destruction and competition, some firms failed, some became successful, and a few have emerged as leading industrial companies.

Most small manufacturing enterprises in these countries have been operating in harsh environments with no formal institutions and limited infrastructure to support them, but their scaling-up and rapid growth often required improvements in the policy and economic environment. The most important policy support is the removal of discriminatory policies including the high bureaucratic hurdles that small and informal firms often face. Creating a more favorable business environment for small and informal firms also requires improvements in general infrastructure, particularly in electricity supply, road conditions, and communication. Moreover, broad-based improvements in education, particularly primary and secondary education, have often proved the most important first steps for significantly boosting labor productivity (Hayami 1998; Ayele et al. 2009). In summary, recognizing the importance of these homegrown SMEs for the transformation process, and hence for improving the environment in which these enterprises operate, should have high priority for the government.

5. The Domestic Service Sector Supports Economywide Growth, and Export Services Have Important Knowledge Spillover Effects

The service sector plays a supporting role in transformation. Our model simulations demonstrate the significant contribution of the service sector in helping Ghana to achieve MIC status. Ghana also has the potential to develop export services, such as tourism and business services. For example, Indian-style call centers in Accra have long been discussed but will require a set of initial conditions, such as fast and affordable Internet connection and electricity. However, this type of export-oriented subsector is currently very small compared with domestic-oriented services. Thus, although developing these services can make an important contribution to development and is likely to have significant spillover effects, it is unlikely to drive structural transformation.

It is important to note that the benefits of service-sector growth are not limited to exports. Our simulations demonstrate that greater economywide growth can be stimulated through the expansion of domestic services, especially in the trade and transport sectors. It is the strong growth linkages of the service sector that explain, at least in part, why countries such as China and Thailand have experienced more rapid service-sector growth alongside industry-led transformations. In addition, improvements in the service sector's productivity also enhance productivity in other sectors. Unleashing growth in the service sector, in fact, will require removing many of the barriers discussed in the context of FDI inflows and manufacturing development.

6. Unleashing Agricultural Growth Requires Improvement of Farmers' Business Climate

Agricultural growth will play an important role in economic transformation. Our simulation results show that by closing the existing yield gaps in crops, together with achieving comparable productivity growth in the livestock sector, Ghana will reach 6 percent average annual agricultural growth over the next 10 years. The achievable yields underlying these results are based on field trials that have been conducted with an optimal package of inputs. However, the use of such inputs on farms is still low in Ghana.[3] Thus, increasing fertilizer use is commonly believed to be key to closing the yield gap in Ghana, particularly for grain crops such as maize.[4] One important reason for the low use of fertilizer is that farmers face high costs. There are many factors along the fertilizer distribution chain that can affect farmgate prices. A recent study by the International Center for Soil Fertility and Agricultural Development (IFDC 2007) shows that the free-on-board (FOB) price is already relatively high for the main fertilizer products Ghana imports due to the lack of market sophistication and historic ties to a particular product. In addition, the retail price of fertilizer is 40 percent higher than the FOB price including preinspection costs. The costs along the distribution chain include ocean freight charges, taxes and levies, port charges, charges for bagging and stor-

---

[3] According to the GLSS5, conducted in 2005-06 (GSS 2007), only 19 percent of rural households reported the use of fertilizer (Quiñones and Diao forthcoming).
[4] The government has recently announced plans to double fertilizer use in Ghana (*Business Week*, March 31, 2010).

age, importer costs, importer margins, inland transport charges, distributor warehouse and distributor costs, distributor margins, retail transport charges, retail finance costs, other retail costs, and retail margins. Along the distribution chain, transportation costs, both international and domestic, are the largest item. This finding is consistent with evidence from other African countries such as Benin, Madagascar, and Malawi where transport costs account for 50-60 percent of marketing costs (Fafchamps, Minten, and Gabre-Madhin 2005). The high transportation costs relate to the conditions of physical infrastructures such as ports and roads and to the lack of storage warehouses. In addition, institutional arrangements and barriers such as inefficient checking systems along the road and the opportunity for corruption created by the bad road conditions and management contribute to high farmgate prices. As a result, in many African countries farmers must sell about twice as much grain as Asian and Latin American farmers to buy the same amount of fertilizer (Morris et al. 2007, in World Bank 2007c). At the same time and for the same reasons, farmers receive low prices for their products. In Ghana the farmgate price of maize in many places is only half the retail price in Accra (World Bank 2007c).

Fertilizer plays an important role in increasing agricultural productivity, yet the efficiency of its use is determined by many other factors. The GLSS5 survey indicates that although the use of fertilizer is low, the differences in maize yields between two groups of farmers with and without fertilizer use is insignificant (GSS 2007). The only significant difference in yields is related to herbicide use; with herbicide use, maize yields come close to two metric tons per hectare, the level identified as the achievable yield by the government (Quiñones and Diao forthcoming). The modest impact of fertilizer use on maize yields is also confirmed by Banful (2009), who assesses the government's recent fertilizer subsidy program in Ghana. These results caution against overemphasizing the importance of fertilizer as a silver bullet. Rather, they confirm the findings from other studies that stress the importance of a comprehensive approach to increasing agricultural productivity sustainably. This has to include a focus on improving rural roads to reduce the prices of inputs (fertilizer and pesticides), refocusing extension services and training extension agents to spread knowledge of improved land management and farm practices, and encouraging more research and development to provide high-yielding seed varieties to the market.

The high yield response of maize to the use of herbicides in Ghana also seems to indicate another constraint on improving agricultural productivity, labor supply, particularly during land preparation, weeding, and harvesting. Herbicide is a substitute for the labor of weeding and is also important for improving yields (or preventing yield losses). In a relatively land-abundant country like Ghana, dominated by smallholder agriculture, labor constraints will become increasingly important due to both demand for and supply of labor. Increasing crop yields often requires additional labor inputs for certain farm practices. At the same time, a significant increase in yields often requires additional labor for harvesting. A recent study by Nweke (2009) confirms this for some areas of Nigeria and Ghana, where significant yield increases in cassava production have forced farmers to limit their cassava production areas due to labor shortages. Labor supply-side factors are related to rural–urban migration, which is expected to further speed up in the process of transformation. To address both seasonal and permanent labor constraints, mechanization has a long history in Ghana and has recently been revived by the government as a possibility to foster intensification. However, the GLSS5 survey shows that only 7 percent of rural households have rented equipment (mainly tractor services) at the national level, and this percentage is higher in two agroecological zones (GSS 2007). In these zones, the landholding size of the farmers who use tractors is twice as great as that of the farmers who do not use equipment (Quiñones and Diao forthcoming).

Ghana's recent policy of advancing mechanization emphasizes the importance of public–private partnerships. The government supports the import of equipment by providing credit to private tractor service centers, and the service centers provide fee-based tractor services to farmers. However, given that there has been an intense debate about the merits of mechanization and how it should be promoted (see Pingali 2007 and Mrema 2008 for extensive reviews of this topic), it is worth revisiting the main arguments from this literature in order to provide practical policy suggestions.

Increasing agricultural productivity through the promotion of modern technologies is commonly referred to as a Green Revolution. There is no doubt that launching a Green Revolution requires a significant increase in public investments in agriculture, rural roads, and market infrastructure. However, the economywide returns from such investments are high. Our simulations show that by taking into account both visible and invisible transfers from agriculture to the nonagricultural economy, a Green Revolution type of agricultural development will provide huge benefits to the economy. Measured in monetary terms, the total financial transfers from agriculture to the rest of the economy are equivalent to 13 percent of the GDP increase expected in the next 10 years.

Growth in agricultural productivity also results from promoting new activities and exploring additional market opportunities that increase the value addition of agricultural production. For example, the recent spike in global energy prices has led to foreign investments in biofuel production; the FAO projects that Ghana will be among the greatest producers of the biofuel plant jatropha in Africa by 2015 (FAO and IFAD 2010). At the same time, the spike in global food prices has encouraged the private sector to invest in agro-industries in Africa, including Ghana.[5] As in the case of manufacturing, it is important to enhance the linkages between foreign investment in agriculture and the rest of the sector and the rural economy in order to foster spillover effects. For example, outgrower schemes have stronger linkage and poverty reduction effects than do plantations, a finding that needs to be considered when governments negotiate with investors (Arndt et al. 2008). Supporting rural producer groups is another area in which the government can play an important role, including through capacity-building for leaders to manage and participate in high-level negotiations and for the weaker members of the groups to achieve a voice within the groups. Promoting modern information and communication systems helps enable producer groups to access market information and acquire the professional advice necessary for modern supply chain management and effective participation in the policy dialogue (World Bank 2007c).

Opportunities also exist for structural change within the agricultural sector and hence for increasing agricultural productivity through diversification. With rising rural and urban incomes and rapid urbanization, many agricultural products move from subsistence to marketed crops. A recent study by Robinson and Kolavalli (2010), for example, shows that imports of processed tomato products offer opportunities to develop import substitution manufacturing that can support crop diversification. An important policy question is what supportive role the state can play in this process. Lessons from successful examples of public–private initiatives, such as the development of the salmon industry in Chile, may help to provide practical policy advice.

The findings of this monograph emphasize that agricultural development is not only important for transformation but is also key to further poverty reduction in Ghana. Agricultural growth benefits the whole economy through strong linkages between the agricultural sectors and the rest of the economy. In this process, the incomes of both rural and urban households increase, and the resulting additional demand for agricultural products can be met by domestic supply without significantly lowering their prices. Agricultural growth, particularly growth that is broad based, such as Green Revolution–type growth, is also pro-poor. At the national level, the model scenario shows that the national poverty rate will fall to 12.5 percent by 2015, lifting an

---

[5] For example, according to local newspapers, the Indian Farmers Fertilizer Cooperative is building a fertilizer plant in Ghana, and FDI in food processing from India and other countries is increasing.

additional 850,000 people out of poverty compared to the baseline. However, our results also show that poverty levels in North Ghana remain high, indicating the need for additional and targeted measures in this region beyond those of a Green Revolution.

7. Ghana May Need an Industrial Policy

To conclude, we raise the question of whether Ghana needs an industrial policy. This monograph has focused on the country's economic transformation as a process of development. It emphasizes that transformation is not only about structural change in the sense of changing the relative importance of economic sectors. Structural change also involves producing new goods with new technologies and transferring resources from traditional activities to new ones (Rodrik 2007). Thus, this monograph raises important questions regarding the role of the state versus the market in transformation in Ghana. In the process of transformation, private entrepreneurs starting new businesses in agriculture and other sectors take special risks and rely on an environment conducive to innovations and start-ups. If they succeed, these new businesses create jobs and generate positive externalities through technological spillovers, learning by doing, and strong linkage effects. However, the business environment is not always favorable for entrepreneurs and thus often constitutes an important market imperfection.

Addressing such market imperfections requires government action. The Washington Consensus emphasized the principles "stabilize, liberalize and privatize," and although applying these principles to countries has often led to improved macroeconomic stability, it has by and large failed to promote private-sector-driven growth and transformation in Ghana and elsewhere (Easterly 2001; Rodrik 2006). Rethinking transformation as a development process therefore requires emphasizing the importance of actively stimulating the dynamic forces behind the growth process and paying more attention to country-specific factors (World Bank 2005). From this point of view, industrial policies may play an important role in stimulating growth and structural change. The theoretical justification for industrial policy is strong, but the empirical evidence as to whether industrial policy works or what kind of industrial policy works is inconclusive.

Answers to the question of whether Ghana needs an industrial policy can be inspired by a review of industrial policies in three non-Asian settings and related arguments by Rodrik (2007). The development literature raises a number of valid concerns about the likely shortcomings of industrial policy in practice, especially the inability of governments to "pick winners" due to informational imperfections, corruption, and rent-seeking (Balassa 1971; Pack and Saggi 2006). Yet Rodrik argues that none of these makes industrial policy different from conventional areas of government responsibility such as education, health, social insurance and safety nets, infrastructure, or stabilization. In each of these areas, policy discussions typically focus on how to make things work, not on *whether* the government should be involved in the first place. Thus making progress toward answering the question of whether or not an industrial policy can help accelerate transformation requires a similar shift. Although the specifics of industrial policy design depend on the circumstances and the institutional capacities of a country, the right model for industrial policy should be a model of strategic collaboration and coordination between the private sector and the government. The aim should be to uncover the most significant bottlenecks to private-sector-led development and to design the most effective interventions accordingly, periodically evaluating the outcomes and learning from the mistakes being made in the process. Active government involvement works when governments "adopt a pragmatic, gradual exit that provides transitory protection to the old priority sectors in order to maintain stability, and liberalizes sectors consistent with the economy's comparative advantages so as to achieve dynamism simultaneously" (Lin 2010, 19). The Government of Ghana has a unifying, politically salient vision of transforming the country in the next 10–15 years. To realize this vision, the government also needs to have a systematic, proactive strategy for implementation.

Gross National Income per Capita in the Study Countries

Table A.1   Gross national income (GNI) per capita for the 17 middle-income developing countries (current 2005 US$)

Region, country	Year with GNI around US$200	GNI (US$)	Year with GNI around US$1,000	GNI (US$)	Number of years required to become a middle-income country
Latin America					
Brazil	1960	208	1975	1,128	15
Dominican Republic	1960	205	1980	1,123	20
Costa Rica	1960	377	1976	1,111	16
El Salvador	1960	241	1992	1,102	32
Paraguay	1965	211	1989	1,087	24
Mexico	1960	343	1974	1,233	14
Asia					
China	1982	201	2001	1,027	19
India	1978	203	2005	731	
Indonesia	1974	204	1995	1,018	21
Malaysia	1960	289	1977	1,050	17
Philippines	1972	205	1995	1,114	23
Sri Lanka	1973	217	2005	1,182	32
Thailand	1972	213	1988	1,144	16
Vietnam	1994	221	2005	615	
Africa					
Egypt	1970	216	1996	1,086	26
Morocco	1963	214	1990	1,038	27
Tunisia	1961	202	1979	1,050	18

Source: Calculated from World Bank (2008).
Note: India and Vietnam had not yet reached middle-income-country status by 2005.

Growth and Structural Change

Table B.1   Ghana's gross domestic product by economic activity (as a percentage of total), 1970-2007

Activity	1970-72	1973-83	1984-93	1994-2000	2001-07
Agriculture, hunting, forestry, fishing	41.7	54.3	41.2	36.8	38.0
Mining, manufacturing, utilities (combined)	12.5	6.4	13.4	17.3	16.3
Manufacturing	10.1	5.2	8.9	9.1	8.6
Construction	4.1	1.9	4.1	8.1	7.7
Trade, restaurants, and hotels	11.7	20.8	7.9	6.2	6.4
Transport, storage, and communication	4.0	3.2	4.9	4.2	4.3
Other activities	15.9	8.2	19.4	18.4	18.9
Total	100.0	100.0	100.0	100.0	100.0

Source: Calculated from World Bank (2008).

Table B.2   Ghana's exports (as a percent of total), 1965-2006

Export	1965-72	1973-83	1984-93	1994-2000	2001-06
Manufactures	0.8	1.3	4.2	14.7	19.5
Ores and metals	15.9	15.1	10.1	12.1	5.4
Agricultural raw materials	11.2	8.0	8.8	11.7	6.6
Food (including cocoa)	71.5	70.5	70.3	56.3	64.2
Fuel	0.7	4.9	6.6	5.1	4.2
Other exports	0.1	0.1	0.0	0.1	0.2
Total	100.0	100.0	100.0	100.0	100.0

Source: Calculated from World Bank (2008).

Table B.3   Ghana's imports (as a percent of total), 1965-2006

Import	1965-72	1973-83	1984-93	1994-2000	2001-06
Manufactures	71.1	60.1	59.2	65.1	67.6
Ores and metals	1.8	1.7	0.6	0.8	1.6
Agricultural raw materials	1.4	2.0	1.6	2.0	1.5
Food	18.0	13.1	9.5	11.1	16.9
Fuel	6.4	19.1	26.1	18.2	12.2
Other imports	1.2	4.0	3.1	2.8	0.1
Total	100.0	100.0	100.0	100.0	100.0

Source: Calculated from World Bank (2008).

Table B.4   Ghana's average annual gross domestic product (GDP) growth by economic activity, 1965-2006

Activity	1965-72	1973-83	1984-93	1994-2000	2001-06
Agriculture	4.9	-0.2	2.0	4.3	3.8
Industry	4.1	-6.7	4.8	4.8	7.9
Services	1.0	0.0	7.9	4.3	6.3
GDP	3.5	-1.2	4.7	4.4	5.5
GDP per capita	1.3	-3.5	1.8	1.9	3.2

Source: Calculated from the World Bank (2008).

Table B.5   Ghana's gross domestic product by expenditure (as a percent of total), 1965-2007

Expenditure	1965-72	1973-83	1984-93	1994-2000	2001-07
Final consumption expenditure	89.9	95.6	94.6	92.8	91.5
Household consumption expenditure	75.9	87.8	82.5	82.9	76.9
General government final consumption expenditure	14.0	7.9	12.1	10.0	14.5
Gross capital formation	12.4	4.7	14.6	22.7	29.4
Gross fixed capital formation	12.4	4.8	14.9	22.4	29.4
Changes in inventories	0.0	-0.1	-0.3	0.4	0.0
Net trade	-2.3	-0.3	-9.2	-15.6	-20.9
Exports of goods and services	18.4	6.4	17.0	35.1	38.9
Imports of goods and services	20.7	6.7	26.2	50.7	59.8
Total	100.0	100.0	100.0	100.0	100.0

Source: Calculated from World Bank (2008).

Table B.6   Ghana's population and employment, 1965-2006

Measure	1965-72	1973-83	1984-93	1994-2000	2001-06
Population (percent of total)					
Rural	71.9	69.1	64.4	57.4	53.3
Urban	28.1	30.9	35.6	42.6	46.7
Largest city	6.1	7.6	7.5	8.1	8.8
Urban >1 million	9.5	11.5	11.5	13.6	15.5
Population growth (annual average)					
Rural	1.5	2.0	1.8	1.1	0.8
Urban	4.0	3.2	5.0	4.3	3.9
Total	2.2	2.4	2.9	2.4	2.2
Employment by sector (percent of total)					
Agriculture	64.0	58.0	61.1	62.0	55.0
Industry	14.0	17.0	12.8	10.1	14.0
Services	22.0	25.0	26.1	27.9	31.1

Source: World Bank (2008).
Note: Data on employment by sector 1960-80 from Boateng (1997), in Aryeetey and Fosu (2002).

Table B.7   Ghana's public expenditure for selected sectors (average share in total), 1979-2006

Sector	1979-83	1984-93	1994-2000	2001-06
Education	20.5	23.6	18.5	17.7
Health	6.9	8.7	5.1	9.6
Agriculture, forestry, fishing, hunting	11.5	3.8	1.9	4.3
Mining and minerals	2.1	1.2	2.1	2.3
Roads, waterways, transport, communication	6.8	9.6	11.4	9.5
Other spending	52.3	53.1	61.0	56.6
Total	100.0	100.0	100.0	100.0

Source: Unpublished data from Ghana Statistical Services.

Major Political and Economic Events in Ghana

Table C.1   Chronology of major political and economic events in Ghana, 1895-2008

Year	Event(s)
1895	Cocoa exports begin.
1951	"Self-rule" begins. New constitution grants internal self-government. Nkrumah elected prime minister.
1957	Independence achieved. Nkrumah elected prime minister.
1960	Ghana becomes a republic with Nkrumah as president.
1964	Single-party government by Convention People's Party (CPP) begins.
1966	Military coup replaces Nkrumah and establishes National Liberation Council (NLC) with A. Africa as chairman.
1969	Elections held. Elected government led by K. Busia.
1972	Military coup overthrows Busia government and establishes National Redemption Council (NRC) with I. K. Acheampong as chairman.
1975	Acheampong replaces NRC with all-military Supreme Military Council (SMC).
1978	SMC replaces Acheampong with F. Akuffo.
1979	New elections held after Rawling attempts coup. H. Liman elected president.
1981	New coup by Rawling establishes Provisional National Defense Government.
1983	Economic Recovery Program launched.
1992	Rawling elected president.
1993	Rawling takes office as president.
2001	Kufuor becomes president after free and fair elections.
2008	Atta Mills is elected president in a run-off election.

Sources: Authors' compilation based on Leith (1996, 7) and various media sources.

APPENDIX D

Model Disaggregation and Equations

Table D.1 Sectors/commodities in the Ghana computable general equilibrium model

Agriculture	Industry	Industry (continued)
Cereal crops	Mining	Electrical machinery
Maize, rice, sorghum/millet	Gold	Televisions
Other cereals	Other mining	Medical appliances
Root crops	Food processing	Vehicles
Cassava, yams, cocoyams	Formal food processing	Vehicle parts
Other staple crops	Informal food processing	Other technical equipment
Cowpeas, soybeans	Cocoa processing	Other equipment
		manufacturing
Groundnuts	Sugar processing	Other industry
Fruits (domestic)	Dairy product processing	Construction
Vegetables (domestic)	Meat and fish processing	Water
Plantains, other crops	Other manufacturing	Electricity
Export crops	Textiles	Services
Palm oil, other nuts	Clothing	Private
Other nuts, fruits (export)	Leather and footwear	Trade services
Vegetables (export)	Wood products	Export services
Cocoa beans	Paper, publishing and printing	Transport services
Industrial crops	Crude and other oils	Communication
Livestock	Petroleum	Banking and business
Chickens (broilers)	Diesel fuel	Real estate
Eggs and layers	Other fuels	Public and community
Beef	Fertilizers	Community, other
		services
Sheep and goat meat	Chemicals	Public administration
Other meats	Rubber products	Education
Forestry	Other nonmetal products	Health
Fishery	Machinery	

Source: Authors.

Table D.2 Mathematical presentation of the dynamic computable general equilibrium model: Sets, parameters, and variables

Symbol	Explanation	Symbol	Explanation
Sets			
$a \in A$	Activities	$c \in CMN(\subset C)$	Commodities not in CM
$c \in C$	Commodities	$f \in F$	Factors
$c \in CD(\subset C)$	Commodities with domestic sale of domestic output	$i \in I$	Institutions (domestic and rest of world)
$c \in CDN(\subset C)$	Commodities not in CD	$i \in ID(\subset I)$	Domestic institutions
$c \in CE(\subset C)$	Exported commodities	$i \in IDNG(\subset ID)$	Domestic nongovernment institutions
$c \in CEN(\subset C)$	Commodities not in CE	$h \in H(\subset IDNG)$	Households
$c \in CM(\subset C)$	Imported commodities	$r \in R$	International trading regions
Equation parameters			
$cwts_c$	Weight of commodity c in consumer price index	$shif_{if}$	Factor income distribution shares
ica_{ca}	Quantity of intermediate input c per unit of activity a	$shii_{ii'}$	Share of institution i's income paid to institution i
$ice_{c'c}$	Quantity of commodity c as trade input per exported unit of c'	ta_a	Indirect tax rate on activity a
$icm_{c'c}$	Quantity of commodity c as trade input per imported unit of c'	$tins_{i'}$	Direct tax rate on institution i
$inta_a$	Quantity of aggregate intermediate input per activity unit	tm_c	Import tariff rate on commodity c
α_a^{va}	Shift parameter for production function	tq_c	Indirect sales tax rate on commodity c
α_c^{ac}	Shift parameter for output aggregation function	$trnsfr_{ii'}$	Transfer from institution i' to institution i
α_c^q	Shift parameter for Armington import function	δ_c^t	Export transformation function share parameter
α_c^t	Shift parameter for export transformation function	δ_{fa}^{va}	Production function share parameter

(continued)

Table D.2 Continued

Symbol	Explanation	Symbol	Explanation
β^a	Sectoral capital mobility factor	γ_{ch}	Subsistence demand quantity for commodity c by household h
β_{ch}	Marginal consumption spending on commodity c by household h	θ_{ac}	Yield of output c per unit of activity a
δ_{ac}^{ac}	Share parameter for output aggregation function	ρ_a^{va}	Production function exponent
δ_c^q	Armington import share parameter	ρ_c^{ac}	Output aggregate function exponent
ν_f	Capital depreciation rate	ρ_c^q	Armington import function exponent
α_{fa}^{vaf}	Shift parameter for output aggregation function	ρ_c^t	Export transformation function exponent
iva_a	Quantity of aggregate value-added input per activity unit	η_{fat}^a	Sector share of new capital

Exogenous variables

Symbol	Explanation	Symbol	Explanation
$fsav$	Foreign savings (in foreign currency units)	qg_c	Public consumption spending on commodity c
mps_i	Base savings rate of institution i	$qinvbar_c$	Base year quantity of investment demand
pwm_c	World import price of commodity c	$wfdist_{fa}$	Wage distortion factor for factor f in activity a
pwe_c	World export price of commodity c	qfs_f	Total factor supply for factor f
$qdst_c$	Quantity of stock change for commodity c	cpi	Consumer price index

Endogenous variables

Symbol	Explanation	Symbol	Explanation
WF_f	Return to factor f	$QINT_{ca}$	Intermediate demand for commodity c in activity a
$IADJ$	Investment demand adjustment factor		

Symbol	Definition	Symbol	Definition
EG	Total government expenditure	$QINV_c$	Investment demand for commodity c
EH_h	Total household consumption spending	QM_c	Import quantity for commodity c
EXR	Exchange rate	PA_a	Producer price for activity a
$GSAV$	Government savings	PD_c	Demand price for commodity c
QF_{fa}	Sector demand for factor f in activity a	PE_c	Export price for commodity c
QH_{ch}	Household consumption demand for commodity c	$PINTA_a$	Aggregate intermediate price for activity a
PM_c	Import price for commodity c	QVA_a	Aggregate value-added quantity for activity a
PQ_c	Composite supply price for commodity c	QX_c	Output quantity for commodity c
PVA_a	Aggregate value added price for activity a	$QXAC_{ac}$	Quantity of commodity c from activity a
PX_c	Aggregate producer price for commodity c	$TRII_{ii'}$	Total transfer from institution i' to institution i
$PXAC_{ac}$	Producer price of commodity c from activity a	YF_f	Total income for factor f
QA_a	Quantity of activity a output	YG	Total government income
QD_c	Quantity of domestic output sold domestically	YI_i	Total income of institution i
QE_c	Export quantity for commodity c	YIF_{if}	Income from factor f paid to institution i
QQ_c	Composite supply quantity for commodity c	ΔK^a_{fat}	Quantity of new capital allocated to activity a
$QINTA_a$	Aggregate intermediate demand quantity in activity a	AWF^a_{ft}	Average economy-wide return for factor f
		PK_{ft}	Capital price for capital stock f in time period t

Source: Authors.

Table D.3 Mathematical presentation of the dynamic computable general equilibrium model: Model equations

Production and price equations

$$QINT_{ca} = ica_{ca} \cdot QINTA_a \tag{1}$$

$$PINTA_a = \sum_{c \in C} PQ \cdot ica_{ca} \tag{2}$$

$$QVA_a = a_a^{va} \cdot \left(\sum_{f \in F} \delta_{fa}^{va} \cdot \left(\alpha_{fa}^{vaf} \cdot QF_{fa} \right)^{-\rho_a^{va}} \right)^{-\frac{1}{\rho_a^{va}}} \tag{3}$$

$$WF_f \cdot wfdist_{fa} = PVA_a \cdot QVA_a \cdot \left(\sum_{f' \in F} \delta_{f'a}^{va} \cdot \left(\alpha_{f'a}^{vaf} \cdot QF_{f'a} \right)^{-\rho_a^{va}} \right)^{-1} \cdot \delta_{fa}^{va} \cdot \left(\alpha_{fa}^{vaf} \right)^{-\rho_a^{va}} \cdot (QF_{fa})^{\rho_a^{va}-1} \tag{4}$$

$$QVA_a = iva_a \cdot QA_a \tag{5}$$

$$QINTA_a = inta_a \cdot QA_a \tag{6}$$

$$PA_a \cdot (1 - ta_a) \cdot QA_a = PVA_a \cdot QVA_a + PINTA_a \cdot QINTA_a \tag{7}$$

$$QXAC_{ac} = \theta_{ac} \cdot QA_a \tag{8}$$

$$PA_a = \sum_{c \in C} PXAC_{ac} \cdot \theta_{ac} \tag{9}$$

$$QX_c = \alpha_c^{ac} \cdot \left(\sum_{a \in A} \delta_{ac}^{ac} \cdot QXAC_{ac}^{-\rho_c^{ac}} \right)^{\frac{1}{(\rho_c^{ac}-1)}} \tag{10}$$

$$PXAC_{ac} = PX_c \cdot QX_c \cdot \left(\sum_{a \in A} \delta_{ac}^{ac} \cdot QXAC_{ac}^{-\rho_c^{ac}} \right)^{-1} \cdot \delta_{ac}^{ac} \cdot (QXAC_{ac})^{\rho_c^{ac}-1} \tag{11}$$

$$PE_c = pwe_c \cdot EXR - \sum_{c' \in C} PQ_{c'} \cdot ice_{c'c} \tag{12}$$

$$QX_c = \alpha_c^t \cdot \left(\delta_c^t \cdot QE_c^{\rho_c^t} + (1 - \delta_c^t) \cdot QD_c^{\rho_c^t} \right)^{\frac{1}{\rho_c^t}} \tag{13}$$

$$\frac{QE_c}{QD_c} = \left(\frac{PE_c}{PD_c} \cdot \frac{1 - \delta_c^t}{\delta_c^t} \right)^{\frac{1}{(\rho_c^t-1)}} \tag{14}$$

$$QX_c = QE_c + QD_c \tag{15}$$

$$PX_c \cdot QX_c = PE_c \cdot QE_c + PD_c \cdot QD_c \tag{16}$$

Table D.3   Continued

Production and price equations (cont.)

$$PM_c = pwm_c \cdot (1 + tm_c) \cdot EXR + \sum_{c' \in C} PQ_{c'} \cdot icm_{c'c} \tag{17}$$

$$QQ_c = \alpha_c^q \cdot \left(\delta_c^q \cdot QM_c^{-\rho_c^q} + \left(1 - \delta_c^q\right) \cdot QD_c^{-\rho_c^q} \right)^{-\frac{1}{\rho_c^q}} \tag{18}$$

$$\frac{QM_c}{QD_c} = \left(\frac{PD_c}{PM_c} \cdot \frac{\delta_c^q}{1 - \delta_c^q} \right)^{\frac{1}{(1+\rho_c^q)}} \tag{19}$$

$$QQ_c = QD_c + QM_c \tag{20}$$

$$PQ_c \cdot (1 - tq_c) \cdot QX_c = PD_c \cdot QD_c + PM_c \cdot QM_c \tag{21}$$

$$cpi = \sum_{c \in C} PQ_c \cdot cwts_c \tag{22}$$

Institutional incomes and domestic demand equations

$$YF_f = \sum_{a \in A} WF_f \cdot wf\,dist_{fa} \cdot QF_{fa} \tag{23}$$

$$YIF_{if} = shif_{if} \cdot YF_f \tag{24}$$

$$YI_i = \sum_{f \in F} YIF_{if} + \sum_{i \in IDNG} TRII_{ii'} + trnsfr_{igov} \cdot cpi + trnsfr_{irow} \cdot EXR \tag{25}$$

$$TRII_{ii'} = shii_{ii'} \cdot (1 - mps_{i'}) \cdot (1 - tins_{i'}) \cdot YI_{i'} \tag{26}$$

$$EH_h = \left(1 - \sum_{i \in IDNG} shii_{ih}\right) \cdot (1 - mps_h) \cdot (1 - tins_h) \cdot YI_h \tag{27}$$

$$PQ_c \cdot QH_{ch} = PQ_c \cdot \gamma_{ch} + \beta_{ch} \cdot \left(EH_h - \sum_{c' \in C} PQ_{c'} \cdot \gamma_{c'h}\right) \tag{28}$$

$$QINV_c = IADJ \cdot qinvbar_c \tag{29}$$

$$EG = \sum_{c \in C} PQ_c \cdot qg_c + \sum_{i \in INSDNG} trnsfr_{igov} \cdot cpi \tag{30}$$

$$YG = \sum_{i \in IDNG} tins_i \cdot YI_i + \sum_{C \in CM} tm_c \cdot pwm_c \cdot QM_c \cdot EXR + \sum_{c \in CM} tq_c \cdot PQ_c \cdot QQ_c + trnsfr_{gov\,row} \cdot EXR \tag{31}$$

(continued)

Table D.3   Continued

System constraints and macroeconomic closures

$$QQ_c = \sum_{\alpha \in A} QINTA_a + \sum_{h \in H} QH_{ch} + qg_c + QINV_c + qdst_c \tag{32}$$

$$\sum_{\alpha \in A} QF_{fa} = QFS_f \tag{33}$$

$$YG = EG + GSAV \tag{34}$$

$$\sum_{c \in CM} pwm_c \cdot QM_c = \sum_{c \in CE} pwe_c \cdot QE_c + \sum_{i \in INSD} trnsfr_{irow} + f\,sav \tag{35}$$

$$\sum_{i \in IDNG} mps_i \cdot (1 - tins_i) \cdot YI_i + GSAV + f\,sav \cdot EXR = \sum_{c \in C} PQ_c \cdot QINV_c + \sum_{c \in C} PQ_c \cdot qdst_c \tag{36}$$

Factor accumulation and allocation equations (applies to capital only)

$$AWF_{ft}^a = \sum_{a \in A} \left(\frac{QF_{fa}}{QFS_f} \cdot WF_{ft} \cdot wfdist_{fat} \right) \tag{37}$$

$$\eta_{fat}^a = \frac{QF_{fat}}{qfs_{ft}} \cdot \left(\beta^a \cdot \left(\frac{WF_{ft} \cdot wf\,dist_{fat}}{AWF_{ft}^a} - 1 \right) + 1 \right) \tag{38}$$

$$\Delta K_{fat}^a = \eta_{fat}^a \cdot \left(\sum_{c \in C} PQ_{ct} \cdot qinvbar_{ct} \right) \cdot PK_{ft}^{-1} \tag{39}$$

$$PK_{ft} = \sum_{c \in C} PQ_{ct} \cdot \frac{qinvbar_{ct}}{\sum_{c' \in C} qinvbar_{c't}} \tag{40}$$

$$QF_{f\,at+1} = QF_{f\,at} \cdot \left(1 + \frac{\Delta K_{f\,at}^a}{QF_{f\,at}} - \upsilon_f \right) \tag{41}$$

$$QFS_{ft+1} = QFS_{ft} \cdot \left(1 + \frac{\sum_{a \in A} \Delta K_{f\,at}^a}{QFS_{ft}} - \upsilon_f \right) \tag{42}$$

Source: Authors

APPENDIX **E**

Elasticities Applied in the Model

Table E.1   Elasticities in value-added, Armington import, and constant elasticity of transformation export functions

Sector, subsector	Elasticity in CES value-added	Elasticity for import function substitution (in CES Armington function)	Elasticity for export substitution (in CET function)
Agriculture			
Cereals	0.75	2.6-8.9	
Root crops	0.75		
Other staples	0.75	3.7	4.0
Export crops	0.75	6.5	6.5
Livestock	0.75	6.0	4.0
Fishery and forestry	0.75	2.5-5.0	4.0-5.0
Industry			
Mining	0.75	6.0	6.0
Construction	0.75		
Agriculture-related manufacturing	0.75	5.2-8.8	4.0-8.1
Other manufacturing	0.75	5.9-10.4	1.0-7.7
Other industry	0.75		
Services			
Private	0.75		
Export-oriented	0.75	6.5	6.5
Public	0.75	4.0	4.0

Source: Ghana dynamic computable general equilibrium model.
Note: CES means constant elasticity of substitution; CET means constant elasticity of transformation.

Table E.2   Household budget shares and income elasticities (percent)

Budget items	Current budget share		Marginal budget share		Income elasticity	
	Urban	Rural	Urban	Rural	Urban	Rural
Foods	43.5	52.0	34.6	49.0	0.8	0.9
Maize	0.8	1.8	0.4	1.2	0.4	0.7
Rice and wheat	3.7	4.3	2.6	4.4	0.7	1.0
Root crops	3.0	2.6	2.2	3.3	0.7	1.3
Other staples	7.2	8.6	5.2	7.3	0.7	0.8
Plantains	1.2	1.1	0.9	1.3	0.8	1.3
Chicken	1.6	1.1	2.0	1.5	1.2	1.3
Other livestock	10.8	15.6	8.5	14.4	0.8	0.9
Fish	1.9	2.1	1.8	2.3	1.0	1.1
Other foods	13.3	14.7	10.9	13.2	0.8	0.9
Nonfoods	46.1	37.0	56.6	40.0	1.2	1.1
Clothing	10.4	11.0	8.9	11.0	0.9	1.0
Other manufactures	7.0	9.6	6.9	9.7	1.0	1.0
Fuels	3.8	5.1	8.0	3.5	2.1	0.7
Durable equipment	9.4	4.8	20.9	7.6	2.2	1.6
Water and electricity	0.5	0.1	0.7	0.2	1.4	2.1
Services	25.4	17.4	20.0	19.0	0.8	1.1

Source: Authors' estimates using GSS (2007).

APPENDIX F

Sensitivity Tests

W e focused our sensitivity test on the model results of scenario 5, the combined scenario. Specifically, we conducted four sensitivity tests. In test 1 we cut the elasticity in the Armington functions for imports by 50 percent (that is, reducing the elasticity from its original value at the commodity level by half) to test how sensitive import substitution is in explaining the model results. In test 2 we cut the elasticity in the CET functions for exports by 50 percent to test the sensitivity of export substitutions. In test 3 we doubled the elasticity of substitution between factor inputs in the production function (from 0.75 to 1.5). In the last test, instead of doubling the elasticity of the production functions as we did in test 3, we lowered the value by 50 percent to 0.4. For each test, we reran the model with all other assumptions the same as in the combined scenario.

Table F.1 reports the test results for some variables expected to be most sensitive to the choices of various elasticities. As the table shows, however, the model is very robust to changes in the values of elasticities in both the trade and the production functions. For example, halving the elasticities used in the trade functions changes the GDP per capita of 2015 by about $0 or $5 compared with the results from the original scenario. Lowering the elasticity values in the production function causes a decrease of GDP per capita of $15 by 2015 from the original simulation result. This is the largest deviation from the original results observed in all tests, but the difference is equivalent to only 1.6 percent of the total. We observed similar modest changes for the other variables, as reported in Table F.1. Given this robustness to changes in key elasticities to different levels in the model, we have confidence in the model results.

Table F.1   Sensitivity analysis

Measure	Original combined scenario	Test 1: Armington[a]	Test 2: Constant elasticity of transformation[a]	Test 3: High[b]	Test 4: Low[c]
		Trade function		Production function	
GDP per capita in 2015 (current US$)	956	956	951	970	941
Average annual GDP growth, 2006-15 (%)					
Total	7.6	7.6	7.6	7.7	7.6
Agriculture	6.9	6.9	6.9	7.2	6.5
Industry	8.9	8.8	8.8	8.8	9.1
Services	7.4	7.4	7.4	7.4	7.4
Exports (sector share of total, %)					
Agriculture	48.9	49.3	50.7	50.7	47.0
Industry	36.9	36.5	37.3	36.0	38.0
Services	14.1	15.0	14.3	13.3	15.0
Imports (sector share of total, %)					
Agriculture	5.9	5.7	5.7	5.8	6.2
Industry	85.8	86.0	86.1	85.8	85.7
Services	14.1	15.0	14.3	13.3	15.0
Investment to GDP ratio (%)	38.3	38.7	38.5	37.6	39.5
Sources of growth (%)					
Labor	22.3	22.3	22.3	21.6	22.9
Capital	7.4	7.4	7.5	8.6	5.8
Land	24.5	24.7	24.6	23.5	26.2
Total factor productivity	45.8	45.6	45.7	46.3	45.2

Source: Authors.
Note: GDP means gross domestic product.
[a]50 percent lowered substitution elasticities.
[b]Doubling substitution elasticities.
[c]50 percent lowered substitution elasticities.

References

Agyeman-Duah, I., ed., with C. Kelly. 2008. *An economic history of Ghana: Reflections on a half-century of challenges and progress.* Banbury, U.K.: Ayebia Clarke.

Akoto-Osei, A. 2008. Part two: A vampire economy with a silver lining. In *An economic history of Ghana: Reflections on a half-century of challenges and progress,* ed. I. Agyeman-Duah with C. Kelly. Banbury, U.K.: Ayebia Clarke.

Alesina, A., and E. La Ferrara. 2005. Ethnic diversity economic performance. *Journal of Economic Literature* 43 (3): 762–800.

Anderson, K., and W. A. Masters. 2007. *Distortions to agricultural incentives in Africa.* Agricultural Distortions Working Paper 56. Washington, D.C.: World Bank.

Arndt C., R. Benfica, F. Tarp, J. Thurlow, and R. Uaiene. 2008. *Biofuels, poverty, and growth: A computable general equilibrium analysis of Mozambique.* IFPRI Discussion Paper 803. Washington, D.C.: International Food Policy Research Institute.

Arrow, K. J. 1962. The economic implications of learning by doing. *Review of Economic Studies* 29 (2): 155–173.

Aryeetey, E. 2008. Part one: Structures and institutions in a postcolonial economy. In *An economic history of Ghana: Reflections on a half-century of challenges and progress,* ed. I. Agyeman-Duah with C. Kelly. Banbury, U.K.: Ayebia Clarke.

Aryeetey, E., and A. Fosu. 2002. Explaining African economic growth performance: The case of Ghana. Report prepared for the African Economic Research Consortium. African Economic Research Consortium, Nairobi, Kenya.

Auty, R. M. 1990. *Resource-based industrialization: Sowing the oil in eight developing countries.* Oxford, U.K.: Clarendon.

———. 1993. *Sustaining development in mineral economies: The resource curse.* London: Routledge.

Ayele, G., J. Chamberlin, L. Moorman, K. Wamisho, and X. Zhang. 2009. *Infrastructure and cluster development: A case study of handloom weavers in Ethiopia.* ESSP-II Discussion Paper 1. Washington, D.C.: International Food Policy Research Institute.

Balassa, B. 1971. *The structure of protection in developing countries.* Baltimore: Johns Hopkins University Press.

Banful, A. B. 2009. *Operational details of the 2008 fertilizer subsidy in Ghana: Preliminary report.* GSSP Background Paper 18. Washington, D.C.: International Food Policy Research Institute.

Barthel, F., M. Busse, and R. Osei. 2008. *The characteristics and determinants of FDI in Ghana.* HWWI Research Paper 2-15. Hamburg, Germany: Hamburg Institute of International Economics.

Berry, L. V. 1993. Ghana, a country study. Federal Research Division, Library of Congress, Washington, D.C. <http://lcweb2.loc.gov/frd/cs/ghtoc.html>. Accessed July 2009.

Bloom, D. E., and J. G. Williamson. 1998. Demographic transitions and economic miracles in emerging Asia. *World Bank Economic Review* 12 (3): 419–455.

Boateng, K. 1997. Institutional determinants of labour market performance in Ghana. Research paper. Centre for Economic Policy Analysis, Accra, Ghana.

Bogetic, Y., M. Bussolo, X. Ye, D. Medvedev, Q. Wodon, and D. Boakye. 2007. Ghana's growth story: How to accelerate growth and achieve MDGs? Background paper for Ghana Country Economic Memorandum. World Bank, Washington, D.C.

Breisinger, C., and X. Diao. 2008. *Economic transformation in theory and practice: What are the messages for Africa?* IFPRI Discussion Paper 797. Washington, D.C.: International Food Policy Research Institute.

Breisinger, C., X. Diao, and J. Thurlow. 2009. Modeling growth options and structural change to reach middle income country status: The case of Ghana. *Economic Modeling* 26 (2): 514–525.

Breisinger, C., J. Thurlow, and M. Duncan. 2007. *A 2005 social accounting matrix (SAM) for Ghana.* Accra, Ghana, and Washington, D.C.: Ghana Statistical Services and International Food Policy Research Institute. <http://www.ifpri.org/dataset/ghana>. Accessed September 2, 2010.

Breisinger, C., X. Diao, J. Thurlow, and R. Al Hassan. 2009. Potential impacts of a green revolution in Africa: The case of Ghana. *Journal of International Development.* Published online November 23. DOI: <http://dx.doi.org/10.1002/jid.1641>. Accessed November 3, 2010.

Brinkerhoff, D. W., and A. A. Goldsmith. 2005. Institutional dualism and international development: A revisionist interpretation of good governance. *Administration and Society* 37 (4): 199–224.

Brooks, J., A. Croppenstedt, and E. Aggrey-Fynn 2007. *Distortions to agricultural incentives in Ghana.* Agricultural Distortions Working Paper 47. Washington, D.C.: World Bank.

Cato, A. A. 2008. Part one: Structures and institutions in a postcolonial economy. In *An economic history of Ghana: Reflections on a half-century of challenges and progress,* ed. I. Agyeman-Duah with C. Kelly. Banbury, U.K.: Ayebia Clarke.

Chenery, H. B. 1960. Patterns of industrial growth. *American Economic Review* 50 (4): 624–654.

Chenery, H. B., and L. Taylor. 1968. Development patterns among countries and over time. *Review of Economics and Statistics* 50 (4): 391–416.

Chinery-Hesse, M. 2008. Part one: Structures and institutions in a postcolonial economy. In *An economic history of Ghana: Reflections on a half-century of challenges and progress,* ed. I. Agyeman-Duah with C. Kelly. Banbury, U.K.: Ayebia Clarke.

Christiaensen, L., L. Demery, and J. Kuhl. 2006. *The role of agriculture in poverty reduction: An empirical perspective.* World Bank Policy Research Working Paper 4013. Washington, D.C.: World Bank.

Chuta, E., and E. Liedholm. 1979. *Rural nonfarm employment: A review of the state of the arts*. Rural Development Paper 4. East Lansing, Mich., U.S.A.: Michigan State University.

Coady, D., M. Grosh, and J. Hoddinott. 2004. *The targeting of transfers in developing countries: Review of experience and lessons*. Washington, D.C.: World Bank and International Food Policy Research Institute.

Delgado, C., J. Hopkins, V. Kelly, P. Hazell, A. McKenna, P. Gruhn, B. Hojjati, J. Sil, and C. Courbois. 1998. *Agricultural growth linkages in Sub-Saharan Africa*. Research Report 107. Washington, D.C.: International Food Policy Research Institute.

Dervis, K., J. de Melo, and S. Robinson. 1982. *General equilibrium models for development policy*. New York: Cambridge University Press.

Diao, X., J. Rattsø, and H. E. Stokke. 2005. International spillovers, productivity growth and openness in Thailand: An intertemporal general equilibrium analysis. *Journal of Development Economics* 76 (2): 429–450.

Diao, X., P. Hazell, D. Resnick, and J. Thurlow. 2007. *The role of agriculture in development: Implications for Sub-Saharan Africa*. Research Report 153. Washington, D.C.: International Food Policy Research Institute.

Djurfeldt, G., H. Holmen, M. Jirström, and R. Larsson. 2005. *The African food crisis: Lessons from the Asian Green Revolution*. Wallingford, U.K.: CABI.

Dutz, M. A. 2007. *Unleashing India's innovation: Toward sustainable and inclusive growth*. Washington, D.C.: World Bank.

Easterly, B. W., and R. Levine. 2003. Tropics, germs, and crops: How endowments influence economic development. *Journal of Monetary Economics* 50 (1): 3–39.

Easterly, W. 2001. The lost decades: Explaining developing countries' stagnation in spite of policy reform 1980-1998. *Journal of Economic Growth* 6 (2): 135–157.

Echevarria, C. 1997. Changes in sectoral composition associated with economic growth. *International Economic Review* 38 (2): 431–452.

Edwin, J., and W. Masters. 2005. Genetic improvement and cocoa yields in Ghana. *Experimental Agriculture* 41 (4): 491–503.

Emerson, C. 1982. Mining enclaves and taxation. *World Development* 10 (7): 561–571.

Evenson, R. E., and D. Gollin. 2003. Assessing the impact of the Green Revolution, 1960 to 2000. *Science* 300 (5620): 758–762.

Fafchamps, M., B. Minten, and E. Gabre-Madhin. 2005. Increasing returns to market efficiency in agricultural trade. *Journal of Development Economics* 78 (2): 406–442.

FAO (Food and Agriculture Organization of the United Nations). 1997. *Irrigation potential in Africa: A basin approach*. Rome.

——. 2008. FAOSTAT database. <http://faostat.fao.org/default.aspx>. Accessed December 2008.

FAO (Food and Agriculture Organization of the United Nations) and IFAD (International Fund for Agricultural Development). 2010. Jatropha: A smallholder bioenergy crop—The potential for pro-poor development. *Integrated Crop Management* 8.

Fei, J. C., and G. Ranis. 1961. A theory of economic development. *American Economic Review* 514: 533–565.

Fisher, A. G. B. 1939. Production, primary, secondary and tertiary. *Economic Record* 15: 24-38.

Freedom House. 2009. Ghana country report. <http://www.freedomhouse.org/template.cfm?page=22&year=2008&country=7400>. Accessed February 2010.

Friis-Hansen, E. 2000. *Agricultural policy in Africa after adjustment.* CDR Policy Paper. Copenhagen, Denmark: Centre for Development Research.

Gelb, A. H., et al. 1988. *Oil windfalls: Blessing or curse?* New York: Oxford University Press.

Ghana, MoFA (Ministry of Food and Agriculture). 2007. *Agriculture in Ghana 2006: Statistics research and information directorate.* Accra, Ghana.

——. 2009. *Agriculture sector plan: 2009-2015.* Accra, Ghana.

Ghana, NDPC (National Development Planning Commission). 2005. *Growth and poverty reduction strategy (GPRS II) 2006-2009.* Accra, Ghana.

Gohin, A. 2005. The specification of price and income elasticities in computable general equilibrium models: An application of latent separability. *Economic Modeling* 22 (5): 905-925.

Goody, J. 1971. *Technology, tradition and the state in Africa.* London: Oxford University Press.

Green R. H. 1987. *Stabilization and adjustment policies and programmes: Country Study 1: Ghana.* Helsinki, Finland: United Nations University-World Institute for Development Economics Research.

Grossman, G., and E. Helpman. 1992. *Innovation and growth in the global economy.* Cambridge, Mass., U.S.A.: MIT Press.

GSS (Ghana Statistical Services). 2007. Ghana Living Standard Survey Round 5 (GLSS5). Accra, Ghana: Ghana Statistical Office.

Gyimah-Boadi, E. 2008. Part three: Crossing the Jordan: Stimulation and innovation in the economy. In *An economic history of Ghana: Reflections on a half-century of challenges and progress,* ed. I. Agyeman-Duah with C. Kelly. Banbury, U.K.: Ayebia Clarke.

Hayami, Y. 1974. Conditions for the diffusion of agricultural technology: An Asian perspective. *Journal of Economic History* 34 (1): 131-148.

——. 1998. *Towards the rural-based development of commerce and industry: Selected experience of East Asia.* EDI Learning Resource Series. Washington, D.C.: World Bank.

Hayami, Y., and V. Ruttan. 1985. *Agricultural development: An international perspective.* Baltimore: Johns Hopkins University Press.

Helpman, E. 2006. Trade, FDI, and the organization of the firms. *Journal of Economic Literature* 44 (3): 589-630.

Hertel, T., D. Hummels, M. Ivanic, and R. Keeney. 2007. How confident can we be of CGE-based assessments of free trade agreements? *Economic Modeling* 24 (4): 611-635.

Hill, P. 1997. *The migrant cocoa-farmers of Southern Ghana: A study in rural capitalism.* Hamburg, Germany: LIT.

Hirschman, A. O. 1958. *The strategy of economic development.* New Haven, Conn., U.S.A.: Yale University Press.

IFDC (International Center for Soil Fertility and Agricultural Development). 2007. Fertilizer supply and costs in Africa. Chemonics and IFDC, Muscle Shoals, Ala., U.S.A.

IMF (International Monetary Fund). 2008. *Ghana selected issues.* IMF Country Report 08/332. Washington, D.C.

———. 2010. Factsheet: Debt relief under the Heavily Indebted Poor Countries (HIPC) Initiative. <http://www.imf.org/external/np/exr/facts/hipc.htm.> Accessed January 6, 2011.

Irz, X., and T. Roe. 2005. Seeds of growth? Agricultural productivity and the transitional dynamics of the Ramsey model. *European Review of Agricultural Economics* 32 (2): 143–165.

Itoh, M., and M. Tanimoto. 1998. Rural entrepreneurs in the cotton weaving industry of Japan. In *Towards the rural-based development of commerce and industry: Selected experience of East Asia,* ed. Y. Hayami. EDI Learning Resource Series. Washington, D.C.: World Bank.

Jayne, T. S., J. Govereh, A. Mwanaumo, J. K. Nyoro, and A. Chapoto. 2002. False promise or false premise? The experience of food and input market reform in eastern and southern Africa. *World Development* 30 (11): 1967–1985.

Jimenez, E. 1995. Human and physical infrastructure: Public investment and pricing policies in developing countries. In *Handbook of Development Economics,* vol. 3, ed. J. R. Behrman and T. N. Srinivasan. Amsterdam, the Netherlands: Elsevier.

Johnson, M., P. Hazell, and A. Gulati. 2003. The role of intermediate factors markets in Asia's Green Revolution: Lessons for Africa? *American Journal of Agricultural Economics* 85 (5): 1211–1216.

Johnston, D. G., and J. W. Mellor. 1961. The role of agriculture in economic development. *American Economic Review* 51 (4): 566–593.

Jorgenson, D. W. 1961. The development of a dual economy. *Economic Journal* 71 (282): 309–334.

Kaufmann D., A. Kraay, and M. Mastruzzi. 2008. *Governance matters VII: Governance indicators for 1996-2007.* Washington, D.C.: World Bank.

Kikushi, M. 1998. Export-oriented garment industries in the rural Philippines. In *Towards the rural-based development of commerce and industry: Selected experience of East Asia,* ed. Y. Hayami. EDI Learning Resource Series. Washington, D.C.: World Bank.

Kilby, P., and C. Liedholm. 1986. *The role of non-farm activities in the rural economy.* Employment and Enterprise Policy Analysis Discussion Paper 7. Cambridge, Mass., U.S.A.: Harvard Institute for International Development.

King, R. P., and D. Byerlee. 1978. Factor intensities and locational linkages of rural consumption patterns in Sierra Leone. *American Journal of Agricultural Economics* 60 (2): 197–206.

Kolavalli, S., K. Flaherty, R. Al-Hassan, and K. Owusu Baah. 2010. *Do Comprehensive Africa Agriculture Development Program (CAADP) processes make a difference to country commitments to develop agriculture? The case of Ghana.* IFPRI Discussion Paper 1006. Washington, D.C.: International Food Policy Research Institute.

Krueger, A. O. 1986. Aid in the development process. *World Bank Research Observer* 1 (1): 57-78.

Krueger, A. O., M. Schiff, and A. Valdes. 1991. *The political economy of agricultural pricing policies.* Washington, D.C.: World Bank.

Kuznets, S. 1955. Economic growth and income inequality. *American Economic Review* 45 (1): 1-28.

——. 1961. *Capital in the American economy.* New York: National Bureau of Economic Research.

——. 1966. *Modern economic growth.* New Haven, Conn., U.S.A.: Yale University Press.

——. 1973. Modern economic growth: Findings and reflections. Nobel Memorial Lecture. *American Economic Review* 63 (3): 247-258.

Leechor, C. 1994. Ghana: Frontrunner in adjustment. In *Adjustment in Africa: Lessons from country case studies,* ed. I. Husain and R. Faruqee. Washington, D.C.: World Bank.

Leith, J. C. 1996. *Ghana: Structural adjustment experience.* International Centre for Economic Growth, Country Study 13. San Francisco: ICS Press.

Lewis, W. A. 1954. Economic development with unlimited supplies of labor. *Manchester School* 22 (2): 139-191.

——. 1979. The dual economy revisited. *Manchester School* 47 (3): 211-229.

——. 1984. The state of development theory. *American Economic Review* 74 (1): 1-10.

Lin, J. 2010. *New structural economics:* A framework for rethinking development. Policy Research Working Paper 5197. Washington, D.C.: World Bank.

Lofgren, H., R. Harris, and S. Robinson. 2002. *A standard computable general equilibrium (CGE) model in GAMS.* Trade and Macroeconomics Discussion Paper 75. Washington, D.C.: International Food Policy Research Institute.

Markusen, J. 2002. *Multinational firms and the theory of international trade.* Cambridge, Mass., U.S.A.: MIT Press.

Markusen, J. R., and A. Venables. 1999. Foreign direct investment as a catalyst for industrial development. *European Economic Review* 43 (2): 335-356.

Matthews, R. C. O. 1986. The economics of institutions and the sources of growth. *Economic Journal* 96 (384): 903-918.

McKay, A., and E. Aryeetey. 2004. Operationalizing pro-poor growth: A country case study on Ghana. A joint initiative of AFD, BMZ (GTZ, KfW Development Bank), DFID, and the World Bank. <http://www.dfid.gov.uk/pubs/files/oppgghana.pdf>. Accessed July 2008.

McLaughlin, J., and D. Owusu-Ansah. 1995. Historical setting. In *Ghana, a country study,* ed. L. V. Berry. Federal Research Division, Library of Congress, Washington, D.C. <http://lcweb2.loc.gov/frd/cs/ghtoc.html>. Accessed September 3, 2010.

Meier, G. M. 1989. *Leading issues in economic development.* New York and Oxford, U.K.: Oxford University Press.

Morris, M., V. Kelly, R. Kopicki, and D. Byerlee. 2007. *Promoting fertilizer use in Africa.* Direction in Development Series. Washington, D.C.: World Bank.

Mrema, C. G., ed. 2008. *Agricultural mechanization policies and strategies in Africa: Case studies from Commonwealth African countries.* Proceedings of a workshop held in Zaria, Nigeria. Nigeria Food Production and Rural Development Division. London: Commonwealth Secretariat.

Navaretti, G., and A. Venables. 2004. *Multinational firms in the world economy.* Princeton, N.J., U.S.A.: Princeton University Press.

Nehru, V., and A. Dhareshwar. 1994. *New estimates of total factor productivity growth for developing and industrial countries.* Policy Research Working Paper 1313. Washington, D.C.: World Bank.

Nweke, F. 2009. Resisting viruses and bugs: Cassava in Sub-Saharan Africa. In *Millions Fed: Proven successes in agricultural development,* ed. David J. Spielman and Rajul Pandya-Lorch. Washington, D.C.: International Food Policy Research Institute.

Nin-Pratt, A., and B. Yu. 2008. *An updated look at the recovery of agricultural productivity in Sub-Saharan Africa.* IFPRI Discussion Paper 787. Washington, D.C.: International Food Policy Research Institute.

——. 2010. Getting implicit shadow prices right for the estimation of the Malmquist index: The case of agricultural total factor productivity in developing countries. *Agricultural Economics* 41 (3-4): 349-360.

Ofori-Atta, K. 2008. Part three: Crossing the Jordan—Stimulation and innovation in the economy. In *An economic history of Ghana: Reflections on a half-century of challenges and progress,* ed. I. Agyeman-Duah with C. Kelly. Banbury, U.K.: Ayebia Clarke.

Ohno, A., and B. Jirapatpimol. 1998. The rural garment and weaving industry in Northern Thailand. In *Towards the rural-based development of commerce and industry: Selected experience of East Asia,* ed. Y. Hayami. EDI Learning Resource Series. Washington, D.C.: World Bank.

Omtzigt, D.-J. 2008. Part one: Structures and institutions in a postcolonial economy. In *An economic history of Ghana: Reflections on a half-century of challenges and progress,* ed. I. Agyeman-Duah with C. Kelly. Banbury, U.K.: Ayebia Clarke.

Osei, R. D. 2008. Part two: A vampire economy with a silver lining. In *An economic history of Ghana: Reflections on a half-century of challenges and progress,* ed. I. Agyeman-Duah with C. Kelly. Banbury, U.K.: Ayebia Clarke.

Osei, R. D., and G. Domfe. 2008. *Oil production in Ghana: Implications for economic development.* ARI 104/2008. Accra, Ghana: Institute of Statistical Social and Economic Research, University of Ghana.

Oteng-Gyasi, T. 2008. Part three: Crossing the Jordan: Stimulation and innovation in the economy. In *An economic history of Ghana: Reflections on a half-century of challenges and progress,* ed. I. Agyeman-Duah with C. Kelly. Banbury, U.K.: Ayebia Clarke.

Pack, H., and K. Saggi. 2006. *The case for industrial policy: A critical survey.* Working Paper 3839. Washington, D.C.: World Bank.

Pearson, L. B. 1969. *Partners in development.* Report of the Commission of International Development. Santa Barbara, Calif., U.S.A.: Praeger.

Pingali, P. 2007. Agricultural mechanization: Adoption patterns and economic impact. In *Handbook of Agricultural Economics,* vol. 3, ed. R. Evenson and P. Pingali. Amsterdam, the Netherlands: North-Holland.

Poulton, C., J. Kydd, and A. Dorward. 2006. Overcoming market constraints on pro-poor agricultural growth in Sub-Saharan Africa. *Development Policy Review* 24 (3): 243-277.

Quiñones, E. J., and X. Diao. Forthcoming. *Understanding patterns of crop production in Ghana: What can we learn from the GLSS5 survey?* GSSP Working Paper. Washington, D.C.: International Food Policy Research Institute.

Robinson, E. J. Z., and S. L. Kolavalli. 2010. *Ghana Strategy Support Program (GSSP).* GSSP Working Paper 20. Washington, D.C.: International Food Policy Research Institute.

Rodrik, D., ed. 2003. *In search of prosperity: Analytic narratives on economic growth.* Princeton, N.J., U.S.A.: Princeton University Press.

———. 2006. Goodbye Washington consensus, hello Washington confusion? A review of the World Bank's economic growth in the 1990s: Learning from a decade of reform. *Journal of Economic Literature* 44 (4): 973-987.

———. 2007. *Normalizing industrial policy.* Working Paper 3 for the Commission on Growth and Development. Washington, D.C.: World Bank. <http://dev.wcfia.harvard.edu/sites/default/files/Rodrick_Normalizing.pdf>. Accessed September 3, 2010.

Rodrik, D., A. Subramanian, and F. Trebbi. 2004. Institutions rule: The primacy of institutions over geography and integration in economic development. *Journal of Economic Growth* 9 (2): 131-165.

Romer, P. M. 1990. Endogenous technological change. *Journal of Political Economy* 98 (5): 71-102.

Schultz, T. W. 1964. *Transforming traditional agriculture.* New Haven, Conn., U.S.A.: Yale University Press.

———. 1968. *Economic growth and agriculture.* New York: McGraw-Hill.

Sen, A. 1998. *Development as freedom.* New York: Knopf.

Stern, N., J. J. Dethier, and F. H. Rogers. 2005. *Growth and empowerment: Making development happen.* Munich Lecture in Economics. Cambridge, Mass., U.S.A.: MIT Press.

Syrquin, M. 1988. Patterns of structural change. In *Handbook of Development Economics,* vol.1, ed. H. Chenery and T. N. Srinivasan. New York: Elsevier.

Syrquin, M., and H. B. Chenery. 1986. *Patterns of development: 1950 to 1983.* Washington, D.C.: World Bank.

Thurlow, J. 2004. *A dynamic computable general equilibrium (CGE) model for South Africa: Extending the static IFPRI model.* TIPS Working Paper 1. Pretoria, South Africa: Trade and Industrial Policy Strategies.

Tiffin, R., and X. Irz. 2006. Is agriculture the engine of growth? *Agricultural Economics* 35 (1): 79-89.

Timmer, P. 2008. *The structural transformation as a pathway out of poverty: Analytics, empirics and politics.* Center for Global Development Working Paper 150. Cambridge, Mass., U.S.A.: Harvard University.

Torvik, R. 2001. Learning by doing and the Dutch disease. *European Economic Review* 45 (2): 285-306.

TradeInvest Africa. 2010. Website. <http://www.tradeinvestafrica.com/>. Accessed April 1, 2010.

UN (United Nations), Statistics Division. 2009. National accounts 1970-2007. <http://unstats.un.org/unsd/snaama>. Accessed January 15, 2009.

UNDP (United Nations Development Programme). 2009. Human Development Index. <http://hdr.undp.org/en/statistics/indices/hdi/>. Accessed January 15, 2009.

Yartei, C. A. 2006. *The stock market and the financing of corporate growth in Africa: The case of Ghana.* IMF Working Paper WP/06/201. Washington, D.C.: International Monetary Fund.

Yergin, D., and J. Stanislaw. 1998. *The commanding heights: The battle for the world economy.* New York: Simon and Schuster.

Young, C. 1994. *The African colonial state in comparative perspective.* New Haven, Conn., U.S.A.: Yale University Press.

Yu, W., T. Hertel, P. V. Prechel, and J. S. Eales. 2003. Projecting world food demand using alternative demand systems. *Economic Modeling* 21 (1): 99-129.

Wilhelmsson, M. 2002. Spatial models in real estate economics. *Housing, Theory and Society* 19 (2): 92-101.

Winters, P., A. de Janvry, E. Sadoulet, and K. Stamoulis. 1998. The role of agriculture in economic development: Visible and invisible surplus transfers. *Journal of Development Studies* 34 (5): 71-97.

World Bank. 2005a. *Expanding opportunities and building competencies for young people: A new agenda for secondary education.* Washington, D.C.

——. 2005b. *Economic growth in the 1990s: Learning from a decade of reform.* Washington, D.C.

——. 2006. *World development report 2007: Development and the next generation.* Washington, D.C.

——. 2007a. Development data and statistics: Country classification. <http://go.worldbank.org/K2CKM78CC0>. Accessed July 2007.

——. 2007b. *Ghana: Meeting the challenge of accelerated and shared growth.* Country Economic Memorandum. Washington, D.C.

——. 2007c. *World development report 2008: Agriculture for development.* Washington, D.C.

——. 2008. World Development Indicators (WDI). <http://www.data.worldbank.org/indicator>. Various access dates.

——. 2009. World Development Indicators (WDI). <http://www.data.worldbank.org/indicator>. Various access dates.

World Bank and IMF (International Monetary Fund). 2009. *Joint IMF and World Bank debt sustainability analysis.* Washington, D.C.: World Bank and International Monetary Fund.

About the Authors

Clemens Breisinger is a research fellow in the Development Strategy and Governance Division of the International Food Policy Research Institute, Washington, D.C.

Xinshen Diao is a senior research fellow in the Development Strategy and Governance Division of the International Food Policy Research Institute, Washington, D.C.

Shashidhara Kolavalli is a senior research fellow in the Development Strategy and Governance Division of the International Food Policy Research Institute, Washington, D.C.

Ramatu Al Hassan is a professor in the Department of Agricultural Economics and Agribusiness of the University of Ghana, Legon.

James Thurlow was formerly a research fellow in the Development Strategy and Governance Division of the International Food Policy Research Institute, Washington, D.C. He is now a research fellow at the United Nations University's World Institute for Development Economics Research, Helsinki, Finland.

Index

Page numbers for entries occurring in figures are suffixed by *f*, those for entries occurring in boxes by *b*, those for entries occurring in notes by *n*, and those for entries in tables by *t*.

FAO. *See* Food and Agriculture Organization
Farmers. *See* Agricultural sector; Smallholder
farmers
FDI. *See* Foreign direct investment
Fei, J. C., 25
Fertility rates, 12, 14t
Fertilizer: imports of, 29; prices of, 103-4;
subsidies of, 104; use of, 103
Food: demand for, 51-52, 78-79, 89; imports
of, 51-52, 84; prices of, 28, 78, 84, 89,
90-91, 104. *See also* Crops
Food and Agriculture Organization (FAO) of
the United Nations, 60, 105-6
Food processing, 57, 78-79
Foreign aid, 59, 71, 97
Foreign direct investment (FDI): in agricul-
ture, 106; attracting, 99-100; in colonial
period, 33b; in Ghana, 41, 45, 47, 71, 99;
inflows during transformation, 27, 28t,
30-31, 99; in manufacturing, 41; spillovers
from, 24, 27, 30-31, 100-101, 106
Forestry products, 33b, 76, 83
Forest Zone, 44, 90. *See also* Agroecological
zones

Garment industries. *See* Textile and clothing
industries
General equilibrium models, 53-54, 55n,
58n. *See also* Dynamic computable general
equilibrium model
Ghana: development strategies of, xv-xvi, 4,
34-35, 37-38, 97-98; economic structure of,
43-44, 43t, 110t, 111t; future challenges
of, 3-4, 47-52; history of, 32-41, 113t;
independence of, 33b, 34, 36; opportunities for transformation in, 47-48; political
system of, 2, 35, 36, 98-99; in preindependence period, 33b; transformation in, xv,
2-3, 42, 46t
Ghana Cocoa Board, 21
Ghana Living Standards Survey (GLSS5), 42,
56, 60, 62, 63, 80, 92, 104, 105
Global economic crisis, 1n
GLSS5. *See* Ghana Living Standards Survey
Gold: exports of, 3-4, 34; foreign investments
in, 41, 99; production of, 33b
Governance, 1-2
Government bonds, Ghanaian, 2, 45
Government policies: on agricultural development, 38-39; implementation of, 98; industrial policy, 107-8; role in transformation,
20, 35, 36, 41; state-led industrialization,
4, 20, 38, 40, 97; supportive of productivity
growth, 96-97; support of manufacturing
growth, xvi. *See also* Policy implications;
Public investment

Government revenues: from cocoa and gold
exports, 2, 3-4, 21, 38; data sources for,
62; from oil, 3, 59, 97; sources of, 38, 97
Government spending: data sources for, 62;
in Ghana, 79-80; revenue sources for, 38;
by sector, 112t
GPRS II. *See* Growth and Poverty Reduction
Strategy, Second
Green Revolution: benefits of, 85; irrigation
in, 23; productivity increases in, 25, 85;
pro-poor growth in, xvii; public investment
in, xvii-xviii, 22, 85, 105; technology
adoption in, 25, 30
Growth and Poverty Reduction Strategy,
Second (GPRS II), 4, 9
Growth scenarios. *See* Scenarios

Heavily Indebted Poor Countries (HIPC)
program, 45, 45n
Herbicides, 104
HIPC. *See* Heavily Indebted Poor Countries
program
Hirschman, A. O., 27
Human capital, 24, 24n, 27, 45-46, 100
Human Development Index, 19

IFDC. *See* International Center for Soil Fertility
and Agricultural Development
IMF. *See* International Monetary Fund
Imports: of agricultural equipment, 105; in
colonial period, 33b; of consumer products,
101; in DCGE model, 57; demand for, 76; of
fertilizer, 29; of food, 51-52, 84; of Ghana,
73t, 111t; growth scenarios and, 72, 73t,
74t, 77t; manufactured, 72, 76; by sector,
74t, 111t
Import substitution, 20, 51, 63, 76, 84, 87,
97, 106
Income distribution: changes due to transformation, 17, 18, 29; costs of increased
inequality, 19; in Ghana, 56; urban-rural,
12; wage rates and, 60-61
Income elasticities, 51-52, 63, 64, 122t
Incomes: by agroecological zone, 91, 92t;
of consumers, 56; growth of, 91-94, 92t;
regional differences in, 44; remittances,
42, 45, 56; of rural population, 78-79;
wage rates, 60-61. *See also* Poverty
India: economic growth in, 9; fertility rates
in, 12; service sector as growth driver in,
10-11; service sector in, 10-11, 79, 100
Indonesia, 10, 11, 12, 77-78
Industrialization: agricultural surplus used in,
26-27; Ghanaian efforts, 37-38, 40; homegrown, 40, 47-48, 49b, 71, 101; import substitution, 20, 97, 106; income inequality